EFFECTIVE EVANGELISTIC PREACHING

EFFECTIVE EVANGELISTIC PREACHING

by
V. L. STANFIELD

BAKER BOOK HOUSE
Grand Rapids, Michigan
1965

Copyright 1965 by
Baker Book House Company

Printed in the United States of America

FOREWORD

In the "preface" to my doctoral dissertation I noted that I had often felt inclined to do the "work of an evangelist." My interest in this area has never diminished.

While teaching has been the primary area of my vocational Christian service, I have been permitted to fulfill the calling to be an "evangelist." It has been my joy and responsibility to participate in more than one hundred seventy-five church revivals. I do not claim to have done the task well, but I have exercised this gift of the Spirit with great joy and always with a desire to learn to do it more effectively.

Since many of my brothers in the ministry have confessed a need for assistance in the area of the evangelistic sermon and especially in the giving of the invitation, I am recording some of the things which I have learned from study in this field, from experience in meetings, and from the counsel of pastors with whom I have served.

Because good examples are more helpful than techniques, I have included sermons from some of the men who are doing the work of an evangelist most effectively. I am grateful to these men who have been willing to share their messages with brother preachers. My own sermon on invitations has been included because it has been used by so many of my students and seems to have met a need.

If these principles, techniques, and messages help in our greatest task, to win men to Christ, my objective will have been fulfilled.

The material in Parts I and II retains the informal lecture style in which it was delivered.

V. L. Stanfield

CONTENTS

PART I. EVANGELISTIC PREACHING 11
   Basic Presuppositions of Evangelistic Preaching 12
   The Central Message of Evangelistic Preaching 16
   The Occasions for Evangelistic Preaching 17
   The Goals of Evangelistic Preaching 19
   The Qualities of Evangelistic Preaching 20
   The Construction of the Evangelistic Sermon 22
   The Delivery of the Evangelistic Sermon 24

PART II. EVANGELISTIC INVITATIONS 27
   The Reasons for Giving Invitations 27
   The Kinds of Invitations 28
   The Marks of Good Invitations 30
   The Methods of Motivation 32
   Some Related Considerations 36

PART III. EVANGELISTIC SERMONS 39
   "Freedom through Truth," Billy Graham 41
   "Getting Down to Business," H. Leo Eddleman 48
   "Who Is a Christian?" Gregory Walcott 55
   "Greatness in the Church," Carl E. Bates 60
   "The Incapacity of God," H. H. Hobbs 66
   "An Invitation Especially for You," V. L. Stanfield 73

BIOGRAPHIES OF CONTRIBUTORS OF MODEL SERMONS

William F. (Billy) Graham was born in Charlotte, North Carolina, received the B.Th. degree from Florida Bible Institute, Tampa, and the A.B. degree from Wheaton College, Wheaton, Illinois. He has honorary D.D. degrees from Wheaton and William Jewell College and LL.D. degrees from Houghton College and Baylor University.

Ordained into the Baptist ministry in 1940, Dr. Graham began the evangelistic Crusades for Christ in 1946, while he was first vice-president of Youth for Christ International.

Dr. Graham, founder and president of Billy Graham Evangelistic Association, has conducted major evangelistic crusades in more than sixteen countries on every continent and in twenty states of the United States. For fifteen years, he has broadcasted a weekly television and radio program, "Hour of Decision," over the major national television and radio networks.

Dr. Graham is recipient of the Bernard Baruch Award, and a Fellow of the Royal Geographic Society.

H. Leo Eddleman, president of New Orleans Baptist Theological Seminary since 1959, is a native Mississippian. He has the Bachelor of Arts degree from Mississippi College and the Master of Theology and Doctor of Philosophy degrees from Southern Baptist Theological Seminary, Louisville, Kentucky.

A missionary to Palestine from 1936-41, Dr. Eddleman has formerly served as professor of Old Testament and Hebrew on the faculties of Southern Baptist Seminary, Louisville, and New Orleans Seminary. He was pastor of Parkland Baptist Church, Louisville, for ten years and was president of Georgetown College, 1954-59.

A popular speaker, Dr. Eddleman has participated in evangelistic crusades around the world. Most recently, he has been to South America and to Thailand, by invitation of the Foreign Mission Board of the Southern Baptist Convention. He is the author of several books, which include: *To Make Men Free*, *The Teachings of Jesus* and *The Second Coming*, a compilation of sermons.

Gregory Walcott, Canoga Park, California, is a movie and television actor and a Baptist layman. Born in Wendall, North Carolina, he attended Mars Hill College and Furman University, and received theatrical training at the Theater of Arts, Hollywood.

Mr. Walcott, a deacon and charter member of First Baptist Church, Beverly Hills, California, has been a Christian since 1952. He was elected second vice-president of the Southern Baptist Convention for 1964-65 and has served as California representative on the Southern Baptist Brotherhood Commission.

Speaking engagements as a Christian layman have taken him from New Orleans to Thailand. Mr. Walcott is presently producing and starring in *The Bill Wallace Story*, a film to be prepared for theatrical release by Logos Productions.

Carl E. Bates, pastor of First Baptist Church, Charlotte, North Carolina, was born and reared in Mississippi. Graduating from Mississippi College, he received the Bachelor of Theology and Master of Theology degrees from Southern Baptist Theological Seminary, Louisville, Kentucky. The honorary degree of Doctor of Divinity was conferred upon him by Baylor University, Waco, Texas, in 1951.

A longtime pastor and denominational leader, Dr. Bates has served First Baptist Church, Leesburg, Florida; First Baptist Church, Texarkana, Texas; and First Baptist Church, Amarillo, Texas. During his ministry at Amarillo, Dr. Bates was elected chairman of the General Board of the Baptist General Convention of Texas, and president of the Baptist General Convention of Texas.

Member of numerous Southern Baptist Convention committees, Dr. Bates was president of the Pastors' Conference of the SBC, 1961-62.

Herschel H. Hobbs, a native of Alabama, was graduated from Howard College, Birmingham, and Southern Baptist Theological Seminary, Louisville, Kentucky, where he earned the Th.M. and Ph.D. degrees.

Pastor of First Baptist Church, Oklahoma City, Oklahoma, for more than sixteen years, Dr. Hobbs has also served churches in Alabama, Kentucky and Louisiana. He is active in denominational work and was president of the Southern Baptist Convention, 1961-63. Dr. Hobbs has also been president of the Southern Baptist Pastors' Conference, and a member of numerous boards and committees, including the Board of Trustees, New Orleans Baptist Theological Seminary.

An outstanding preacher and writer, he is author of ten books, including *Cowards or Conquerors, Studies in Hebrews,* and *Fundamentals of Our Faith.*

Vernon Latrelle Stanfield is a native of Atlanta, Missouri. He received his A.B. degree from Northeast Missouri State Teachers College; the Th.M. and Th.D. degrees from Southern Baptist Theological Seminary, Louisville, Kentucky; and has done additional study at Northwestern University, Columbia University, Union Theological Seminary and Oxford University.

Serving on the faculty of Southern Seminary from 1946-59 as assistant, associate and professor of preaching, Dr. Stanfield has been professor of Preaching at New Orleans Baptist Theological Seminary since 1959. He has been the pastor of churches in Missouri and Indiana and interim pastor of many churches.

Dr. Stanfield, a writer as well as popular speaker, is author of *The Christian Worshiping* (published in 1965) and *The Favorite Sermons of John A. Broadus,* and a contributor to *The Encyclopedia of Southern Baptists.* His articles, dealing mainly with preaching and Christian worship, appear frequently in theological journals and Baptist periodicals.

Part I. EVANGELISTIC PREACHING

Evangelistic preaching is here understood to mean the public proclamation of the gospel of Jesus Christ. It assumes a preacher — the herald, the evangelist, the proclaimer; it takes for granted a congregation, though it may range in size from ten to ten thousand; it also presupposes a place for preaching, whether sanctuary, auditorium, tent, tabernacle, amphitheater, stadium, hillside, river bank, or street corner. A man stands before his fellow men and declares to them the mighty redemptive acts of God in Christ.

Perhaps a more complete definition of evangelistic preaching needs to be given. No one has improved on the definition of evangelism set forth in 1918 in the report of the Archbishop's Committee of Inquiry on the Evangelistic Work of the Church. This committee gave this thoughtful, comprehensive definition of evangelism:

> To evangelize is so to present Jesus Christ in the power of the Holy Spirit, that men shall come to put their trust in God through Him, accept Him as their Savior, and serve Him as their King in the fellowship of His Church.[1]

With slight modification this could also be a definition of evangelistic preaching. The definition would read: Evangelistic preaching is presenting "Jesus Christ in the power of the Holy Spirit, that men may put their trust in God through Him, accept Him as their Savior, and serve Him as their King, in the fellowship of His Church." To my classes and to study groups I have given my own definition of evangelistic preaching. Evangelistic preaching is the proclamation of the good news concerning the redemptive acts of God in Christ, by one who experientially knows Jesus Christ, in order to lead others to receive Christ as their Savior and their Lord. While no definition is really adequate or completely satisfying, any definition reveals the lofty nature of the task and creates a desire in the preacher to perform it more effectively.

In the first simultaneous campaign in 1950, I had an experience which comes to every preacher (perhaps to me more than to others). One night as I preached, I just could not "get going." There was no sense of freedom. I "beat the air" and became "louder and louder,"

---

[1] *Toward the Conversion of England* (Toronto: J. M. Dent and Sons, 1946), p. 1.

and finally stopped in complete frustration. A wonderful congregation redeemed the service by singing the invitation "with the heart and with the understanding," and the Holy Spirit wrought salvation in some who believed. After the service a man spoke to me and asked a question, "Do you know what that sermon reminded me of?" To myself I said, "Perhaps it was not so bad, after all." Hopefully I responded, "What?" "That reminded me of a man chopping wood with a dull axe," was the devastating answer. Being a country boy who had "split" the kindling, "chopped" the wood, and "cut" the sprouts, I "got the picture."

Since then I have been trying to sharpen my evangelistic tools. It seems to me that every man called to preach has some gift as an evangelist. Furthermore, every man should endeavor to improve his native abilities; and thereby, he can exercise his gift more effectiely.

1. *Basic Presuppositions of Evangelistic Preaching*

Before any examination of some of the principles, qualities, and techniques of evangelistic preaching, a consideration of the fundamental affirmations undergirding such preaching may be necessary. Unless a man believes in and is committed to certain basic presuppositions, he is not likely to preach evangelistically. What are these presuppositions?

The first presupposition is: Preaching is God's chief instrument of saving men. It has pleased God by the foolishness of preaching to save those who believe. "And how shall they believe in Him whom they have not heard? And how shall they hear without a preacher?" (Romans 10: 14, NASB). Whenever the gospel of Jesus Christ has been preached, men have been delivered from their sins and have been made whole. For wherever Christ is preached, there he is, and he alone can give his gift of salvation.

Those who will not accept the proposition that preaching is God's chief instrument of saving men may not understand the basic nature of Christian preaching. It is not a man sharing his own ideas, opinions, or even interpretations. It is not a man standing before others parading his knowledge or displaying his ability. Ideally, a Christian preacher is one who stands before his fellow men with God's message; he stands in God's stead and speaks for him. Christian preaching is not even speech about God; it is God speaking. Of course, the preacher is not God, and his voice is not God's; but no man can justifiably accept the title, a herald of God, unless he declares, like the Apostle Paul, that which he had first received. Where the mighty acts of God in Christ are proclaimed, there Christ will be to act again.

The proclamation of the good news has been and will be God's chief means of saving men. Preaching and evangelism are inextricably bound together.

The second presupposition is: Christian preaching must be evangelistic. While evangelism is not a New Testament word, evangel is. This evangel, this good news, is the distinctive element in the Christian message. It is *kerugma* more than *didache* which distinguishes the Christian revelation from other religious systems. Other religions have high ethical concepts, but the Christian faith alone proclaims a gospel of the living Lord.

Therefore, some preaching designated Christian preaching is not really Christian preaching. It is often good advice, it is fine religious talk, it is contemporary speech, but it is not Christian preaching because it omits the evangel. Moreover, some preaching which claims to be evangelistic preaching is not. It is sometimes not even good news. It is bad news about sinful men. Any preaching which lacks the *kerugmatic* note should not be called evangelistic preaching. A sermon which never mentions Jesus Christ is not evangelistic and is not worthy of being proclaimed in a Christian pulpit.

Here is one of the advantages of "preaching the Christian year." In this method the main events in the life and ministry of Jesus will be presented. Faithfully done, the following of the Christian year will keep the "mighty acts" of God before a congregation. However, the use of this method is no guarantee that the gospel will be preached. Scripture may be read without its truth being proclaimed. Gospel events may be presented without application or appeal. However it is done, the gospel note must be sounded. For preaching which does not declare the evangel is not really distinctive Christian preaching.

The third presupposition is: The pulpit is the preacher's greatest opportunity to evangelize. George Sweazey declares, "His pulpit still offers the minister his supreme evangelistic opportunity. No form of communication the church has ever followed can compare with preaching."[2]

This may sound like a strange assertion in an age when many preachers depreciate preaching and when there are those "prophets" who predict the almost immediate decline and death of the pulpit. In

---

[2] George Sweazey, *Effective Evangelism* (New York: Harpers, 1953), p. 159.

spite of these claims it must be asserted that the pulpit remains a great evangelistic opportunity. This is not declared without reason.

Many ministers preach to more unconverted people in each Sunday service than they could possibly see personally during the week. Moreover, those who are witnessed to privately need to respond publicly. Evangelism is never complete until the convert is in the fellowship of the church. Moreover, in the sermon the minister has time to give a reasonable basis for decision. He may plan sermons which augment each other until an adequate basis for commitment has been presented. In addition to this, he has the time to persuade, to beseech, and to appeal. Also, the Spirit of God is present in His body. The fellowship of the church provides an atmosphere for evangelism which cannot be found elsewhere. There are good reasons to assert that the pulpit is still the great evangelistic opportunity.

This assertion concerning the validity of public proclamation does not intend to place it in competition with personal witness. These two methods are complementary. Paul exemplified this in Ephesus when he taught the people "publicly and from house to house." (Acts 20: 20). The wise preacher will do personal work as though this is the only way to win men to Christ. Then he should enter his pulpit and preach like this is the only way to win men to Christ.

The fourth presupposition is: Men not in Christ are lost. They are without God and without hope. They are lost in every sense of this term. They are not where they belong. They no longer have a sense of direction. They cannot find their own way. They are away from the one who loves them. They are away from those seeking them. They are away from "home." They are lost!

Do we really believe that men are lost—lost to themselves and lost to God? Do we believe that this lostness will bring separation from God and that its ultimate end is destruction? Do we believe that men not "in Christ" are away from God? Do we believe that the "wages of sin is death?" Do we believe in the reality of hell for unbelievers? Perhaps every preacher should preach a sermon entitled, "Some Things I No Longer Believe." Do we really believe the scriptural teaching concerning those out of Christ?

On a more positive basis, do we think that Christ came "to seek and to save the lost?" Do we believe that in his salvation they can be found? Do we believe that Christ is the way to God?

Surely, every preacher knows by name those who are lost and those who have been found. In every church community there are those who are as sheep without a shepherd; they are weak, distraught, and helpless. (See Matthew 9: 36). On the other hand, there are those people who have been found. They do have a shepherd. They have entered the abundant life the shepherd gives those in the fold.

To believe that men are lost will start the undershepherd seeking them. Moreover, it will bring a new note of urgency into his preaching. When the preacher knows that men are lost, he no longer can preach nonchalantly or half-heartedly. He must now entreat, appeal, beseech. He will exhort in the hope that some will find the Father and home.

The fifth presupposition is: The gospel is still the power of God for salvation. Paul's declaration, "I am not ashamed of the gospel, for it is the power of God for salvation to everyone who believes." (Romans 1: 16, NASB), is still true. The gospel of Christ has a mighty intrinsic power. When the gospel is proclaimed and when a man hears in faith, the power of the gospel works and salvation is wrought in that man's heart.

Perhaps we have sought to win lost people with our own methods and in our own wisdom. We may have begun almost unconsciously to believe in the power of techniques. But power comes from an Omnipotent God, who releases it when the good news concerning Jesus Christ is believed.

Proof of this fact has come again and again in my own ministry. One incident stands out. I was supplying in a church on Easter Sunday. The service at 8:30 A.M. was the first of three services. I asked the Minister of Education this question, "Who will receive the people who respond to the invitation?" He smiled and said, "We have not had a pastor for several weeks, and this is Easter Sunday. Let's not worry too much." But arrangements were made to receive those who would respond. I preached on a familiar text, but one not commonly used on Easter Sunday, "If you confess with your mouth Jesus as Lord, and believe in your heart that God has raised him from the dead, you shall be saved." (Romans 10: 9, NASB). Three people responded to the invitation. Two of them were a young couple; he came to transfer his letter; she came to confess faith in Christ. After the service the man and his wife waited to speak to me. Here is the gist of the conversation with the man. "We have not been married long. I am a Baptist and my wife is Jewish. We have wanted to talk to a minister. The sermon answered her questions and she wanted to confess her belief in Christ."

The gospel had worked. Its power had come down, and the gift of salvation had been received by this young woman. The gospel is still the power of God for salvation. If peachers were certain of this fact, they would not scoff at "instant evangelism." The "instant" a sinner believes, the power of the gospel brings salvation.

The sixth presupposition is: Something can happen in the act of preaching. Some men have lost faith in preaching. They no longer believe that great life changes can come about as they preach. Many pastors are insisting that no decisions are made in the service which they do not know will be made. In other words, the preaching service is a "decision registration" service. Now, there is nothing wrong with a pastor working and witnessing and knowing that decisions will be made; in fact, this is most helpful to the service and to his spirit. But a pastor should feel that other decisions may be made, that as he preaches, the Spirit of God will use the Word of God to bring about life commitment.

In our day many preachers need to recover their faith in the efficacy of preaching. As the preacher speaks for God, the Spirit of God can work the miracle of salvation. The living Word created the church, and only the living Word can keep life in the church.

2. *The Central Message of Evangelistic Preaching*

Several references have already been made to the evangel or the good news. As has been previously stated, the evangel is the basis for the evangelistic message. However, rather than to assume that this central message is fully understood, perhaps this question should be raised. What is the core message for evangelistic preaching? C. H. Dodd in his definitive little book, *The Apostolic Preaching and its Developments*, has stressed the fact that the *kerugma* is the central message of the apostles. His careful examination from the excerpts of the apostolic sermons reveals the kerugmatic message. Archibald M. Hunter in *The Message of the New Testament* summarizes the apostolic message under these three headings:

(1) "A claim that their message was the fulfillment of Old Testament prophecy."

(2) "A historical exposition setting forth Jesus in his life, death, resurrection, and exaltation."

(3) "A summons to repent and accept the forgiveness of sins in Jesus."[3]

---

[3]*The Message of the New Testament* (Philadelphia: The Westminster Press, 1944), pp. 29-30.

Many other writers join Dodd and Hunter in stressing the absolute centrality of the *kerugma*.

It should be said, however, that the gospels also contain the *didache*, or the ethical teachings of the Christian faith. While the *kerugma* was the message to the non-Chirstian world, the *didache* was the instruction to the church. I feel that Paul had both in mind when he talked about "my gospel." He wanted men to believe in their hearts and to confess Jesus Christ as Lord, but after this acknowledgment he wanted them to live under the lordship of Christ. Today, the evangelistic message must make central the mighty redemptive acts of God in Christ, but it cannot omit stressing the quality of life expected of the confessing Christian.

Several years ago a preacher was flying home following an eight-day revival. He was on a DC3; the weather was "rough;" the plane was jumping up and down; and at times the light plane appeared to be very near the rugged mountain tops. The preacher said to himself, "I wonder what would happen if we got too close?" Then he added to himself, "That is silly. I know what would happen!" As he continued to meditate, he said both to himself and to God, "If we should crash, and I went to be with you and then came back, could I say more in my preaching than I have been saying?" After thinking about this, he then said to his Lord, "Lord, I am ashamed, for if I went to be with you and came back, I could not say any more than I have been saying—than that Jesus Christ lived and died and arose, and now lives to save those who will trust him." This is the central message for all evangelistic preaching. There will never be any other saving message.

3. *The Occasion for Evangelistic Preaching*

Where should evangelistic preaching be done? Quite often to speak of evangelistic preaching is to bring to mind the special evangelistic service. Most Southern Baptist churches have one revival each year, and some churches have two or more special meetings. The revival represents only one of the primary occasions for evangelistic preaching; there are many other occasions.

One of these occasions is the regular services of the church — Sunday morning, Sunday evening, and Wednesday night. These regular services provide excellent evangelistic opportunities. However, some churches need to change the format of the morning worship service and the evening evangelistic service. In many churches in the mid-1960's the evangelistic opportunity is in the morning. Many more prospects are present in the morning service than in the evening service. The Sunday evening congregation will be made up almost completely of church members. Wednesday night may also be used as an evangelistic service. If a church is to have a perennial program of evangelism, it must use the regular services of the church as occasions for evangelism.

Still another occasion may be termed "special periods in the regular services." Some pastors are now setting aside some four to six weeks for evangelistic endeavors. These men preach evangelistic sermons on Sunday and Wednesday during this designated period. This evangelistic preaching is coupled with intense visitation and personal witness. Some churches have found that they win more people during these special periods than they do during revivals. In highly industrialized areas where week-night activities are not well attended, these special periods seem to be meeting an urgent need.

Still another occasion for evangelistic preaching is in Sunday School departments. These services have often been held in Junior and Intermediate departments. They may well be held in Young People's and in Young Adult departments. In some suburban areas there are more evangelistic prospects among young adults than there are among the children. These services need not destroy the lesson period. The twenty to twenty-five minutes generally given to an opening assembly may be utilized. A pastor may preach a ten-minute sermon and still have adequate time for an invitation to the lost to receive Christ.

Another occasion for evangelistic preaching is the Sunday School service. Here the entire Sunday School, from Juniors through Adults, is brought together, usually in the church auditorium. The lesson time is given over to an evangelistic message and an invitation. This kind of service is often used during a revival meeting. Perhaps the pastor should have this kind of service at least once a year at some time other than the revival time. This service should be planned so that the invitation will be completed and the service ended when Sunday School is normally dismissed. Such planning will overcome a common criticism of the Sunday School service.

Still another occasion for evangelistic preaching is the unified service. This is a service which combines the Sunday School time and the worship time. After opening exercises, the Sunday School, Juniors through Adults, is brought together for an evangelistic service. Many evangelistic leaders warmly commend this kind of service because more time is allowed for both the sermon and the invitation. The unified service has been one of the major methods of simultaneous campaigns.

Still another occasion for evangelistic preaching may be termed the "unusual occasion" — the courthouse square, the street corner, the park, the resort, the beach, wherever people are congregated and will listen to the gospel. It could be that our generation will need to utilize the unusual occasion. Unsaved people no longer attend stated services in large numbers. There is every indication that the twentieth-century church must become more mobile. In a highly mobile society the church cannot be stationary. Every possible occasion to preach the gospel must be seized.

4. *The Goals of Evangelistic Preaching* *To Save Souls*

When the evangelistic message is proclaimed, what goals or objectives should the preacher have in mind? It seems that there are at least four important goals.

The first of these is to gain an inner commitment or an inner decision from the unbeliever. After he has preached the gospel, the preacher invites the lost man to believe in Christ, to trust in Christ, or to commit himself to Christ. The unbeliever is asked to believe in what Christ has done for him. Within himself he is consciously to turn to Jesus Christ and to receive him as his Lord and Savior.

The second goal is to get the person who has just made an inner response to make a public acknowledgment of this inner decision. In our churches the people who believe in Christ are asked to "come forward and make a public profession." Though the making of this public confession is sometimes criticized, there seem to be valid reasons for it. For one thing, public confession is taught in the scripture. Jesus said, "Every one therefore who shall confess me before men, I will also confess before My Father who is in heaven." (Matt. 10:32, NASB). Paul said, "With the heart man believeth unto righteousness, but with the mouth confession is made unto salvation." (Romans 10:10). Also, the acknowledgment of faith seems to strengthen that faith. Furthermore, this confession of faith is the beginning of witness. To stand before a congregation acknowledging Christ as Savior is the Christian's first testimony. Lost people should not be asked to come forward and receive Christ. Rather having already received Christ, having made an inner response, they should be asked to come forward and acknowledge this fact.

A third goal is baptism. Having publicly acknowledged his faith, the new convert is to be baptized. The entire Christian world is studying baptism today, and Baptists have a witness to give. The New Testament clearly teaches "believe, confess, and be baptized," and in this order. While baptism does not save, it is a symbol of salvation. In recent years baptism has not been sufficiently stressed. It is important for the new convert to follow the example and command of his Lord and to be baptized.

A fourth goal is active church membership. Evangelism is not complete until the new convert is in the fellowship of the church. The New Testament knows nothing of isolated discipleship. These persons that were saved were added to the church. Though the invitation is sometimes given "to receive Jesus Christ and do what you want to about the church," this invitation has no New Testament precedent. The new believers were added to the church. This is the ultimate goal of evangelism, that those outside the church will be brought into the fellowship of the church.

5. *The Qualities of Evangelistic Preaching*

Several references have been made to preaching and to the message. What qualities should characterize effective evangelistic preaching? First of all, the evangelistic sermon should be biblical in content. If the preacher is to proclaim the mighty redemptive acts of God in Christ, he must go to the record to learn of these wonderful deeds. Considerable evangelistic preaching has not been biblical. It has not only been topical; it has lacked a biblical basis for the topics. The Bible gives us the printed evangel. In one sense, Christian preaching is giving the Bible a voice. The gospel sermon should be based on the written evangel.

Second, the evangelistic sermon should be positive. It should be good news about Jesus Christ. Much that has been called gospel preaching has been "bad" news rather than good news. The gospel is not based upon what men should not do. The gospel is not even about what men should do. The gospel is the good news of what God has done, is doing, and can do in and through Jesus Christ. It is the uplifted Christ who draws men to him.

Third, evangelistic preaching should be clear. The average educational level in the United States is approximately the tenth grade. This means that sermons must be preached which will be understandable at this educational level. Moreover, the prospect is not usually a regular church attendant. The "language of Zion" may not mean much to the man outside the church. The gospel message must be expressed in simple terms. Biblical ideas, clearly expressed, will be acceptable to all listeners. In evangelistic preaching the preacher should strive for transparent clarity.

Fourth, the evangelistic sermon should be comparatively brief. However, there is no standard concerning the length of the sermon. Its length is often determined by the time set aside for the service. Since the invitation is important, the preacher may want to make his sermon fairly brief so there will be sufficient time for the invitation. Quite often the evangelistic sermon should be briefer than other sermons, because the same people are asked to attend the services night after night. A sermon and service of reasonable length will help attendance.

Fifth, an evangelistic sermon should have "emotional" content. This means that the preacher should express his deepest feelings of love and concern for those outside of Christ. A few years ago there were many "sobbing evangelists." Some people were repelled by extreme emotion, but reaction to these "wet handkerchief" preachers has produced the opposite condition. Many preachers hold in check and disguise their true feelings. Since Jesus wept over a city, and Paul wept over his own people, no Christian preacher should be ashamed of genuine emotion. A gospel sermon undergirded by genuine emotion will impress the hearts of men. Quintilian said, "The speaker must be on fire who is anxious to reach the people."

Sixth, an evangelistic sermon should be marked by a sense of urgency. This is closely related to what has just been said. No evangelistic preacher should preach in an off-hand, nonchalant, or "take-it-or-leave-it" manner.

> A preacher was invited to address the inmates of a large penitentiary. The afternoon before he was to speak he paid a visit to the institution. The warden showed him around, and at last they came to the chapel. It was a large auditorium seating about fifteen hundred. "It will be full tomorrow morning, sir," said the officer. It was not the number of seats, but rather the two particular seats on the front row that intrigued the preacher. "Why are these two chairs here in front draped in black?" he asked. The warden replied, "The two men who will occupy those seats tomorrow are under sentence of death. On Monday they go to the electric chair!" "Under sentence of death," repeated the minister quietly. And then he said, "Do I understand that this will be the last service they will ever attend?" "Yes sir," was the reply. "Your sermon will be the last one they will ever hear."
>
> The preacher had seen all he wanted to. He must find a place to be alone and do some quiet thinking. When he reached home, he went to his study, took out the sermon he had prepared, reviewed it, then tore it up! "This is of no use," he said. "It does not meet the need." Then falling on his knees, he prayed, "O God, give me a message for those two men who will be sitting in those draped chairs."[4]

---

[4] R. A. Anderson, *The Shepherd-Evangelist* (Washington, D. C.: Review and Herald Publishing Association, 1950), pp. 190-191.

Because there are "draped chairs" in every congregation, the preacher must preach with a sense of urgency. Richard Baxter once declared, "Few, if any of us, preach with all our might." To be urgent does not necessarily mean to be loud. A man may express real urgency quietly and gently. Do not be afraid to let your concern show.

Finally, the evangelistic sermon should have a mark of authority. If the gospel is being preached by a man who has been saved and who has been called to preach, such preaching should be characterized by "Thus saith the Lord." The common people were attracted to Jesus because he spoke "as one having authority." Do not apologize; do not be hesitant. When you preach the gospel, preach with the attitude, "This I know."

6. *The Construction of the Evangelistic Sermon*

With these qualities of evangelistic preaching before us, let us now consider the structure of the evangelistic sermon. The principles of preaching which should characterize any sermon should also mark the evangelistic sermon. However, certain principles should be kept in mind as the evangelistic sermon is prepared. We have noted that evangelistic preaching should be biblical. This means that every evangelistic sermon should have a text. After the text is chosen, special care should be given the subject. Is it adequate? Does it cover the subject? An exact subject is the key to good organization. Now you are ready for actual preparation.

The first part of the evangelistic sermon to consider is the body. The body or outline is considered before the introduction because the preacher needs to know what he is introducing before he can introduce it properly. Certain points are quite pertinent for an evangelistic sermon outline.

First, the outline should be easy to follow. You have people in church who do not usually attend. You want them to understand; therefore, what you have to say must be easy to follow. This means that it should be simply stated; this means that it should be logical. Make the outline easy to grasp.

Second, the body of the sermon should be orderly. There should be some genuine arrangement of material, not just a mass of material "stacked together." Do you know why some men cannot remember their sermons long enough to preach them? They have a mass of material "pushed" together. They have not developed any special plan or arrangement. The body of the sermon should have a careful plan.

Third, the body of the sermon should adequately develop the subject. Please note that the injunction was not to develop completely; nor was it to develop exhaustively. Before any subject is completely or exhaustively developed, the congregation will be completely exhausted. So about the best the preacher can do is to develop a subject adequately.

Finally, the body of the sermon should move to a climax. In other words, you move to your objective, to the decision which you will ask the people to make. The ultimate aim of an evangelistic sermon is commitment. The sermon should move to this point. An example is a sermon entitled "Admired, Yet Rejected." It is a textual-topical sermon; that is, the outline comes from the text and from the topic. The text is Isaiah 53:3, "He is despised and rejected of men." Here is the outline. (1) He is despised and rejected. (2) He is admired, yet rejected. (3) He should be admired and accepted. This sermon moves to climax and decision. The preacher asks the congregation to love and accept Jesus Christ.

When the body of the sermon is prepared, at least in outline, then the introduction may be planned. The preacher must know what he is introducing to do so properly. Certain qualities should mark the introduction. First, it should endeavor to capture attention. Some of the people present do not attend church services regularly. They may be only mildly interested. Therefore, the preacher needs to incite interest and attention. He may do this with humor; he may do it with common interest material; he may do it with current events. Billy Graham is a master at taking some highly interesting current event and moving from this event to the Scripture. Regardless of method the preacher needs to capture attention.

Moreover, introduction should be fairly brief. The entire sermon should not be "long." Therefore, only limited time can be spent in the sermon introduction. When your friends visit, they do not like to stay on the porch. When people hear a sermon, they do not want to stay in the introduction. Move quickly into the sermon!

Then, the evangelistic sermon introduction should be marked by assurance. This suggestion may be related to delivery. But the preacher should not be hesitant; he should never apologize. The preacher must give the impression of assurance. The good news about Christ should be declared with real assurance.

Special attention should also be given to the evangelistic sermon conclusion. For one thing, it should be appropriate. In a strictly evangelistic sermon the conclusion and the invitation are one. They are not two separate things. However, the emphasis may be different, and the emphasis in a sermon should be the primary thrust of the conclusion. If you are preaching a sermon that is primarily on the idea of rededication, stress rededication in the conclusion. If the sermon is related to the church, the conclusion should call for commitment to the church. If the sermon is a gospel sermon, then the conclusion is the invitation — a call to receive Christ. Let the conclusion be appropriate or fitting.

The conclusion should also be direct. A good conclusion is often characterized by direct appeal. Note the sermons of John A. Broadus. Dr. Broadus was a great scholar and a wonderful teacher, but when he concluded a sermon he was direct. He would say, "O my brother man." George Truett was a master of direct appeal. This seems to be a lost art among many contemporary preachers. While I take no special pride in the sermon, "An Invitation Especially for You," note that the conclusion is direct appeal. Gregory Walcott gives an excellent appeal in the sermon, "Who is a Christian?"

Finally, a sermon conclusion should be marked by strength or intensity. Some men preach so hard and so loud that when they come to the end of a sermon, they do not have anything left. A good baseball pitcher paces himself so that he can pitch nine innings. Likewise, a preacher with good judgment will pace himself so that he will have real strength for the conclusion of the sermon. Intensity does not mean loudness. Some of the most intense sermon conclusions are quiet. But regardless of method, the conclusion should be characterized by real strength.

7. *The Delivery of the Evangelistic Sermon*

One additional aspect of evangelistic preaching deserves consideration, and this is the delivery of the sermon. The same principles which apply to effective sermon delivery apply to evangelistic preaching; however, several factors need to be stressed. How should the evangelistic sermon be delivered?

First, it should be marked by zeal or enthusiasm. Have you every heard a man preaching in an evangelistic meeting, and he preached so easily that he appeared to be nonchalant? If the preacher has no real enthusiasm, the people will not be attracted. Now, this does not mean that the preacher has to be bombastic or extremely loud, but it does mean that he must speak with zeal. Moreover, this enthusiasm should not be a pattern of delivery. Some men begin in what I call "the key of gee whiz," and they end in this manner. A preacher should speak quietly until his inner feelings demand that he speak enthusiastically. When the preacher realizes that the destiny of the human soul is at stake, he cannot speak easily. The concern of his heart should show in his delivery.

Then the evangelistic sermon should be delivered freely. To be delivered freely does not mean "without an offering;" it does mean without notes or without manuscript. Now, I personally believe that all preaching should be without manuscript, but I certainly believe that evangelistic preaching should be. It seems rather incongruous that a preacher would say, "I have good news from God," and he has to look down to read this news. We say to our people, "You can trust God. God will see you through. There is nothing too hard for the Lord." Yet we do not rely on him completely to help in delivering a sermon. Evangelistic preaching should be without "homiletical crutches." With his heart filled with the grace of Jesus Christ, the preacher should preach freely.

Then above all, evangelistic preaching must be completely dependent upon the Holy Spirit. This is true of all preaching, but it is especially true of evangelistic preaching. We can employ the best techniques, but these are only means to an end. We can declare the gospel, but only the Holy Spirit can make it effectual; only he can give new life. So ultimately the preacher does the best he can, and then trusts the Spirit to bring spiritual victories. John Calvin was a gifted scholar; he was a most effective expositor, but he relied upon the Holy Spirit. Before he went into the pulpit, he would pray this simple prayer, "Come, Holy Spirit, come." Often we have not the Spirit, because we ask not for his Presence. As we preach and seek his blessings, then the preaching of the gospel will be the power of God for salvation.

Part II. Evangelistic Invitations

The invitation is closely related to the evangelistic sermon. In fact, the invitation is the conclusion for an evangelistic sermon. The invitation is certainly a most vital part of every evangelistic service.

The exact origin of the invitation as it is currently used in many evangelical churches is not known. Some writers claim that it grew out of the Weslyan revival; others feel it came out of the Great Awakening. Others insist that it evolved from Charles G. Finney's use of the anxious seat and Asahel Nettleton's use of the inquiry room. Other studies would indicate that the invitation came out of the frontier revivals. After the congregations heard the sermons and were exhorted to repentance and faith, the members of the congregation who were concerned were asked to go into an enclosure for further counsel and exhortation. Ultimately, people were asked to come forward in regular church services.

Regardless of its historical origin, the invitation is certainly implied in God's provision of grace. God offers grace to men freely; God offers redemption to all men; the preacher stands in Christ's stead and proclaims this redemption and entreats men to receive it. Since we do give invitations in regular services and in revival services, it may be of some value to us to consider the reasons for giving invitations. Why do we offer invitations?

1. *The Reasons for Giving Invitations*

There are several valid reasons. The first and the most important reason is that to give an invitation is biblical. You find the spirit of invitations throughout the Bible. When the people had wandered away from God, Moses said to them, "Who is on the Lord's side let him come unto me." (Exodus 32:26). Joshua challenged the people. "Choose ye this day whom ye will serve." (Joshua 24:15). Isaiah invited the people, "Ho, every one that thirsteth, come ye to the waters." (Isaiah 55:1). The word "come" was constantly on the lips of Jesus. This is typified in the great invitation, "Come unto me, all ye that labour and are heavy laden, and I will give you rest." (Matt. 11:28). In the last chapter of the last book of the Bible you will find an all-inclusive invitation, "The Spirit and the bride say, Come. And let him that heareth say, Come. And let him that is athirst come. And whosoever will, let him take the water of life freely." (Revelation 22:17). To give an invitation is to catch the spirit of the Bible.

Second, to give invitations is natural. When you preach a gospel sermon, when you preach of Christ's power to save, when you tell of the grace of God and the love of God, it is just natural to say, "He did this for you! Will you believe it?" To give an invitation is inherent in the gospel. When the apostles had proclaimed Christ, then they said, "Repent and be converted." This was a part of their message. While visiting in England, I observed that few preachers, including Baptists, gave invitations. Gospel sermons were preached, but then a closing worship hymn would be announced. Nothing was said about response; no commitment was sought. I left these services with a feeling of frustration. It seemed that something was lacking, that an opportunity had been missed. When you talk about what God has done for man, it seems to be natural to say to those listening, "Will you accept what he has done?"

Then, to give an invitation is essential. It is essential for the people. They are without God and without hope. When they hear this message of reconciliation, they need to be invited to receive it. It is also essential for the preacher. He needs to complete his sermon and lay claim upon the congregation. I do not know about you, but I find it difficult to preach a sermon and then just stop. I always want to ask people to do something in the light of the truth of the sermon. In the invitation the heart of the preacher should call to the hearts of the people.

2. *The Kinds of Invitations*

Since invitations should be given, what kinds my be offered? Invitations fall into two general groups: invitations to the lost, and invitations to Christians.

To lost people there is one primary invitation and that is the invitation to receive Jesus Christ as Lord and Savior. Some preachers are justly accused of preaching a "cheap" gospel because they often say, "Believe, trust, accept Christ," but do not explain what these terms mean. Lost people are exhorted to "become a Christian" without being told what being a Christian actually is. This is why we should appeal to people to receive Christ as Savior and Lord. He is to save them from their sins, but he is to become the Lord of their lives. Moreover, these two things cannot be separated. To receive Christ is to receive him as the Lord of life. If you have never preached a sermon on the "Lordship of Jesus Christ," you should do so. For this is our primary invitation, to ask people to believe, to yield, to surrender, to take Christ as Savior, and to make him the Lord and Master of life.

An invitation akin to this one is to ask those who have believed in Christ to confess this belief and to be baptized. In some communities, especially where there have been many mass meetings or tent meetings, there are people who have made professions, but they have never been baptized and have not been received into the church. These people need to be invited to present themselves to the church as candidates for baptism.

Certain other invitations may also be given. Lost people may be invited to raise their hands if they desire prayer to be offered for them. Lost people may be asked to remain for counsel. The people may be asked to raise their hands if they would like for the pastor and/or the evangelist to visit them. When response to the invitation has been disappointing the people can be urged to go home and think about any decision which needs to be made. Have you ever preached in a service when there were lost people present, and you had preached faithfully and you had entreated urgently, and yet there was no response? Did you share your discouragement and disappointment? Did you say, "I do not know what could be wrong, but something is." Perhaps you should have said, "I know some of you need Christ. Promise me that you will go home and think about this, then come back and make your decision." Thus you leave a service on a note of anticipation.

Invitations are also given to Christian people. One of these invitations is rededication. Christian people are invited to rededicate or reconsecrate their lives. Rededication is one of the greatest needs confronting the Christian church. This invitation is often misunderstood because it means different things to different people. For many people it means that they have fallen into sin. For other people it means that they have fallen into secret sin, though our sins are never as secret as we think. To other people it means that God has become second; something else has taken priority. For still others rededication means a new vision of service. However, the need for rededication is always present and urgent. A preacher should make no apology for calling the people to rededication.

Still another invitation we give to Christians is to transfer membership. This may be done in three ways: by letter, by statement, or by baptism. The most common way to transfer membership is by letter. Southern Baptists now number more than ten million; however, more than three million of these Baptists are non-resident members. This has been the weakest part of our Southern Baptist program; our "transfer membership weeks" have been far from successful. At least a part of the problem has been the attitude of the preachers. We have been eager to receive the other man's member and hesitant to dismiss our own. Except in the case of some downtown churches, the greatest revival that could come to Southern Baptists would be for all the Baptists living near a local church to join it.

Christians may also transfer membership by statement. This means that the person has previously made a profession of faith and has been baptized into the membership of a Baptist church. Occasionally, however, this membership is lost. Membership records may have been destroyed, or the person has joined a church in another denomination, or the member may have faced church discipline. However, those former members may come back into a Baptist church by statement.

Christian people of other denominations may also join a Baptist church by baptism. They have not been scripturally baptized, and they may become members of a Baptist church by becoming candidates for baptism and by being baptized.

Christians are also invited to respond to the call to vocational Christian service. Young people and others are invited to make the service of the church the vocation of life. This invitation should be issued with great care. When I give it, I always say, "If God has been calling you, you will want to surrender to his call." The call of God must be present. Opportunity may be given for a public response to be made to such a call.

Other invitations are also given to Christian people. They may be asked to pray for the unsaved, or to witness to the lost. They may be asked to bring people to the revival or to be faithful in revival attendance.

Many kinds of invitations are given, but there are these four primary invitations: the invitation to the lost to receive Christ as Lord and Savior, the invitation to Christians for rededication, to transfer membership, and for vocational Christian service.

3. *The Marks of Good Evangelistic Invitations*

Having looked at the kinds of invitations, let us consider the qualities of a good evangelistic invitation. How should an evangelistic invitation be given? Several marks are important. First, an invitation should be given clearly. Be certain the people understand the invitation. Explain the meaning of each invitation. For a good many years I made it a practice to take five to eight minutes during one service in a revival to explain the invitations. I found that to be so helpful to the people that I began preaching a sermon on invitations. This explanation helps the Christian people to talk to others about these commitments. It also helps those who make decisions to make intelligent responses. How can you clarify invitations? You may do this by stressing one invitation at a time. If you are emphasizing rededication, really stress this, then add the others. If you are stressing membership, then major on this, and add the other invitations. If your invitation is primarily to the lost, stress this one, and then add the others. You cannot be too clear. Risk being oversimple in order to be transparently clear.

Second, an invitation should be given honestly. Tell the people what you want them to do and have them do this, no more and no less. An invitation should be just as honest as a banker's statement. It should be just as honest as a good man's word. Yet sometimes "progressive invitations" are given. The "revivalist" may say, "How many of you are lost? Will all the lost stand? Now, if you are really lost and are interested in being saved, you come forward." And on and on it goes. If you ask people to come for prayer, pray for them. Be honest. Do not trick people.

Third, an invitation should be given courteously. We believe in freedom of choice. We believe that each man is a free moral agent, that he has a right to make his own decisions. If he has this right, he must be allowed to express it. He may resist the call of God and turn from Christ, but the "inviter" must be courteous to him. Do not bemean. Do not belittle. Do not exert pressure. Treat lost people just like you would treat a guest in your home. Invite and entreat, but be courteous.

Moreover, an invitation should be given confidently. It should be given expectantly and hopefully. We should give the invitation believing that someone will respond. If you do not feel that a response is going to be made, why give the invitation? It would be better not to give an invitation than to give it perfunctorily.

Dr. George W. Truett was one of the greatest examples of a preacher giving invitations with confidence. As he exhorted the congregation, he said, "You will come." Some men today say just the opposite. "Will you not come?" The obvious response is, "Of course not!" Do not give an invitation negatively. Expect the Spirit of God to convict, to convert, and to move the people to response. Give an invitation with expectation.

Again, an invitation should be given earnestly. Invite with all the sincerity you possess. Do not be nonchalant or matter-of-fact when you offer an invitation. If an invitation is worth giving, it is worth giving earnestly and sincerely. Let the earnest desires of your heart show. Do you want a Baptist to bring his letter and help in your church? Then act like it. Do you really want Christians to rededicate life and make new commitments? Show it. Do you care whether the lost receive Christ? Let them sense it. Give an invitation earnestly.

Finally, an invitation should be given pleadingly. The Apostle Paul entreated, beseeched, appealed, pleaded. Perhaps we should not beg people to make spiritual decisions, but there is a difference between begging and genuine pleading. For a man to bring other people to Christ he must be willing to make a fool of himself; he must be willing to lose his self-consciousness and forget himself. He cannot say, "How will this look? What will people think?" If you saw a child on a railroad track and a train was rapidly approaching, would you say quietly, "Honey, a train is coming?" Would you? No, you would not! You would be shouting and running, urging the child to move out of danger. Men are lost in sin, and are in danger of hell. We must forget ourselves and plead with men to make a response to Christ. Don't be ashamed to "plead with them earnestly."

4. *The Methods of Motivation*

The next topic for consideration is motivation. How do you motivate people? After you present the truth, after you preach with certainty and force and positiveness, then how do you move people? It is one thing to put a product on the counter and demonstrate it; it is another thing to sell it. How do you move to action? Please remember that these things are only means to an end. They are not ends in themselves. All of these things are only instruments which God may use. How do you motivate? What methods of motivation will be helpful?

One method is to appeal to basic drives. Perhaps you have studied in the area of social psychology. Some social psychologists develop long lists of these drives. However, most authors will discuss four to ten basic drives. Often the first one listed is self-preservation. This is an innate desire. Can you show a man self-preservation in Christ? You can promise him eternal life, life in Christ which begins now and continues without end. There is real self-preservation in Christ.

Another basic drive is for personal happiness. People want to be happy; happiness is the big quest of our time. But happiness is often not found by those who seek it; it is a gift from God. The Christian knows the most meaningful joy. Are you happy in Christ?

Can Christ make men happy? Christ can fulfill this desire within men.

Another basic drive is for recognition or prestige. How do you appeal to this? Like so many things, this drive must be sublimated. In this day of mechanization millions of people feel a sense of insignificance, but want a sense of recognition; they want a sense of importance. How can you appeal to this desire? A man reaches his highest worth in Christ. God loved and gave his Son for each man. God knows each man. He takes notice of all our needs. To God each man is a person, each man is significant. Christ proved this when he died for all.

Another basic drive is for security. This is closely related to self-preservation. Does Christianity offer men security? It cannot promise men freedom from care or longevity of life, but it can give men security. Jesus declared, "He that cometh unto me I will in no wise cast out." The highest security, eternal security, is found in Christ and only in Christ.

Another basic drive is for freedom. People want to be free, especially young people. Some people feel that the Christian faith puts a man in chains. However, Jesus said, "Ye shall know the truth, and the truth shall make you free." In Christ there is freedom from sin and freedom from anxiety. This is a freedom within bondage for we must surrender to Christ, but it is freedom. An analogy is found in Christian marriage. Marriage is bondage, but within the "marriage bonds" man and woman enter into the highest freedom. When a man yields himself to Jesus Christ, he enters into a new kind of freedom. A man in Christ is free indeed!

Another basic drive is for adventure. People want the new, the bizarre, the adventurous. Can you promise people genuine adventure in Christ? Southern Baptist leaders are disturbed because fewer of our young people are entering Christian service. One reason for this lack of interest in Christian service may be the ministry. Do we give the impression to our young people that we have found real adventure in the Christian ministry? Some of us give the impression that our service is dull and uninteresting, that we serve not under commission but under constraint. Our young people may be repelled by the very men who should be attracting them into the service of Christ. Think of the joy, the thrills, the high adventure which you have had in your ministry. Many Christians will testify to the wonderful adventure they have known in the Christian life. To serve the King of Kings and Lord of Lords is adventure itself.

Again, another basic drive is for satisfaction. People are seeking that which is completely satisfying. Akin to this is the desire for peace, serenity, tranquillity. The deepest kind of satisfaction is in Christ. The most satisfying fact in life is to know that your sins are forgiven, that you are reconciled with God.

Another method of motivation is the use of certain evangelistic appeals. Evangelistic appeals or motive appeals may help hard hearts to soften and be receptive to the invitation to receive Christ. One such appeal is deliverance from sin. Many people carry a burden of sin, a burden of guilt. They may not have a name for this difficulty, but there is a haunting feeling that things are not right. Deliverance and freedom are in Christ. Through Christ there is reconciliation with God.

Another appeal is an innate hunger for God. Every man is concerned about his origin and his destiny. Because man was made in the image of God, there is an inner desire to know God. Jesus Christ is the way to God. A man finds God in Christ.

Another appeal is for the best way of life. Most people want life to count, they want it to be worthwhile, they want it to be the best. The highest, the best way of life is set forth in, by, and through Jesus Christ. When all things are considered, the Christian way is the noblest way to live.

Still another appeal is for the resources of life. For many people today life is too hard; they cannot meet the demands. Where are resources to be found which are equal to our time? These resources are in Jesus Christ, in God revealed in Christ. Any man who wants extra wisdom, extra strength, extra undergirding, can find these vast resources available in Jesus Christ the Lord.

Another appeal is for the best use of influence. The majority of people want to be positive influences. They want to uplift others rather than degrade them. Without Christ no man can have the highest righteousness. He cannot stand for the best. To be in a position to influence others, a man must make a place for Christ.

A many-sided appeal is the desire for the better — the better community, the better home, the better church. There is this almost innate desire for the best. The best communities are those made up of Christian people. The best churches are those that have the interest and support of all the people. Homes that last are those in which both husband and wife have a genuine commitment to Christ. Though this appeal is labeled questionable, it can be used effectively.

Still another appeal is called response to sacrifice. It is easy to respond to someone who has done something in your behalf. Christ has given himself for all men. You should ask people to turn to Christ because of that which he has done for every man.

Another appeal is the answer to life after death. Because of many tragedies we are forced to think of death. Who has the answer? Jesus Christ has. He died, but conquered death, and now lives. He says to all, "I am the resurrection and the life." Christ has the words of eternal life.

Then there is the appeal to fear. George Sweazey insists that this is a questionable appeal. If so, it is found in the Bible. Eternal separation, eternal punishment, judgment, and hell are all presented in scripture. This appeal should not be primary, and it can be overused. But the Bible warns about the wrath of God. The apostle Paul cried, "Knowing the fear of the Lord, we persuade men." (II Corinthians 5:11, NASB).

After you touch on basic drives, after you make these appeals, then you may use a very common principle of persuasion. One principle especially lends itself to the invitation. That principle of persuasion is a good to be gained or an evil to be avoided. The public hears this constantly. For example, the politicians say, "Get the old crowd out. Get us in. They are bad; we are good." The preacher can also use this. He can show that there is an evil to be avoided and a good to be gained in Christ.

Here is a list of contrasts:

1. Assurance .... Fear
2. Fellowship .... Loneliness
3. Purpose .... Lack of meaning
4. Peace .... Inner conflict
5. Strength .... Weakness
6. Certainty .... Uncertainty
7. Changeless .... Changing
8. Forgiveness .... Guilt
9. Heaven .... Hell
10. Eternal life .... Eternal separation
11. Life .... Death
12. At home .... Away from home
13. Manliness .... Cowardice
14. Fair play .... Unfair play
15. Normal .... Abnormal
16. Reasonable .... Unreasonable

These contrasts are particularly helpful in exhortation. The appeal

35

is to accept the good and avoid the evil.

Then you can motivate men by using an epitome example or illustration. To epitomize means to bring to a point. It is helpful to have an example of another doing what you want the people to do, or making the decision you are asking them to make. If another person has taken such a step, it is easier for those listening to respond. It has been done; it can be done.

So you can motivate by using basic drives, by making certain appeals, by using a principle of persuasion, by using an epitome example. These methods are means to an end. They only create openings whereby the Spirit of God may come in and do his work.

5. *Some Related Considerations*

Since the preacher wants to give the invitation effectively, he has an unusual interest in it. In evangelism classes and in evangelistic conferences many practical questions are raised by the "evangelists." Since some of the questions keep recurring, it may prove helpful to attempt to answer those questions most frequently asked.

One question which often arises is, "Who should give the invitation?" The invitation should be given by the man who has preached the sermon. Since the invitation is the conclusion to an evangelistic sermon, the man who has preached the sermon should best be able to give the invitation. Now some pastors seem to object to this pattern. They want the evangelist to preach, but they want to exhort or to invite. When a man has been invited to be an evangelist, he should be allowed to function. However, I generally say to a pastor whom I am assisting in a meeting, "If you would like to take up the invitation after it is well begun, do so." But notice that I said, "After it is well begun." Some pastors allow the evangelist to begin the invitation, but after one stanza of the invitation hymn, the pastor will "stop the music," exhort the people, and take over the invitation. I doubt that this is the best procedure. The evangelist should give the invitation, and he actually should be responsible for most of it. I really feel that the pastor and evangelist should serve as a team. Sometimes after one invitation hymn, I may say to the pastor, "You know these people better than I do. Perhaps you would like to add to the invitation." I have been in a few invitations where I have exhorted as long as I could. Then I have asked the pastor to continue the invitation. Occasionally I have taken the invitation up again. There is a place in the invitation for both the pastor and the evangelist. The pastor knows the congregation and may be able to say just the right word. However, the evangelist should be in charge of the invitation.

Another question frequently asked is, "How long should an invitation be?" There is no one answer to this question. Some people wish that an exact time could be set. Some few assert dogmatically that the invitation should be brief. However, the length of the invitation is dependent upon many factors, such as the attitude of the church, the prospects present, the spirit of the service, and the leadership of the Holy Spirit. As a general rule I gauge the length of the invitation by the response. If there is interest and response, I extend the invitation. If there is little response, I do not extend the invitation. I find that a long invitation without response brings criticism concerning the invitation. But I also find a thirty-minute invitation will not be criticized when there is real response.

Some invitations are too brief. I find that the longer invitation, lengthened by exhortation as well as by singing, may help prospects to decide for Christ. So I try to plan a revival service so there will be time for the sermon and also for the invitation. This requires cooperative planning on the part of the pastor, the song leader, and the evangelist. The well-planned service allows ten to fifteen minutes for an invitation. When the "long" invitation comes, it will not be criticized if lost people are trusting Christ and if other spiritual decisions are being made.

Another question which often arises is, "How can you move smoothly into the invitation?" Again, there is no "pat" answer, but a variety of ways may be used. Some men offer the invitations, announce the hymn, and then repeat the invitations. The organist and/or pianist will be ready to strike a chord and to begin the hymn. Some pastors and evangelists will use the choir to sing the invitation hymn. The invitations are made and the people are asked to respond while the choir sings. This is a good method. I personally like a combination of these methods. I like to have a congregation sing, because many congregations can sing an invitation in a compelling fashion. Congregations need to be trained to sing invitations. As a part of the elaborate preparation for revivals, congregations should practice singing invitation hymns. After the congregation has sung a hymn, the choir may be used to extend the invitation. The choir may sing a theme hymn which the people come to know and love. The use of both congregation and choir contributes to variety and smoothness. Occasionally a gifted soloist may sing the invitation. This can be a most effective method when the soloist can sing with compassion.

However, I feel that we can over-emphasize smoothness and

over-magnify the danger of hindrances. When the Holy Spirit moves in a man's heart, he will come forward in spite of handicaps.

Still another question which often arises is, "Who should receive the people who respond to the invitation? Here there is a definite answer. All things being considered, the pastor should receive the people who respond. This is especially true during a revival. The evangelist should remain in the pulpit and continue the invitation, and the pastor can receive those who come forward. In regular Sunday services the pastor should probably leave the pulpit in order to receive those persons who respond to his invitation. If a church has other staff members, it may be appropriate to have some staff member other than the pastor to receive the people; however, this should be the exception and not the rule. People like to be received by the pastor, but more than this he should hear their response and thus be able to evaluate the decision which has been made. It is hoped that many people will respond to every invitation and that the pastor will give each one a sincere and meaningful reception.

Part III. Evangelistic Sermons

Counsel on effective evangelistic preaching should be linked to examples of good evangelistic sermons. Thus, it was considered appropriate to include evangelistic sermons in this study. These sermons are from Southern Baptist preachers who are actively engaged in evangelistic meetings. Billy Graham is the great mass evangelist of our time, and perhaps of all time. H. H. Hobbs is not only a pastoral evangelist but is also the Baptist Hour preacher, whose evangelistic message has been and is being heard by multitudes. Gregory Walcott, a lay preacher and a motion picture and television actor, is conducting successful evangelistic meetings. The other men are pastors or teachers who also do the work of an "evangelist."

A sermon loses much of its appeal when separated from the preacher proclaiming it. Nonetheless, these sermons are contemporary in approach, biblical in content, and direct in their appeal. A careful study and analysis of these sermons should add to effectiveness in evangelistic preaching.

1. Billy Graham

Freedom Through Truth
John 8:31-36

Several years ago we toured the various countries of Africa. At that time we were the guests of the Vice-President of Liberia, Dr. Tolbert. In every country we were conscious of one word—"freedom." I remember when we got off the plane in Uganda and Ruanda, we were met at the airport. They thought we were the United Nations delegation that was expected, and thousands of people were shouting, "Freedom, freedom, freedom, freedom." In the march on Washington we heard one word that was used constantly, "Freedom, freedom." All over the world there is a tremendous search for freedom.

Winston Churchill once said, "Freedom is our greatest gift, and we must be ready to die to preserve it."

The late President Kennedy said, "Our freedoms today are threatened."

A Supreme Court Justice said, "Freedom is diminishing all over the world, and a paradox of our time is this, that in a time when people want freedom, are seeking freedom more than any other period in history, freedom is disappearing in the world.

There are many who believe that freedom is disappearing in the United States. In my opinion, which is neither Republican nor Democrat, the encroachment of government with higher and higher taxes all the time is a symptom of our national illness. Gradually every phase of our life is coming under the control of government. Freedom is disappearing, at a time when the whole world is longing for freedom.

Centuries ago, our Lord had something to say about freedom. Turn with me to John's Gospel, chapter eight. "Then said Jesus to those Jews which believed on him, If ye continue in my word, then are ye my disciples indeed; and ye shall know the truth and the truth shall make you free. They answered him, We be Abraham's seed, and were never in bondage to any man: how sayest thou, Ye shall be made free? Jesus answered them, Verily, verily, I say unto you, Whosoever committeth sin is the servant of sin. And the servant abideth not in the house for ever: but the Son abideth ever. If the Son therefore shall make you free, ye shall be free indeed." (John 8:31-36). "Ye shall know the truth, and the truth shall make you free."

The world is longing for political freedom. We are seeking intellectual freedom. We want to know about the universe and so we send men into space. We are going to spend twenty billion dollars to go to the moon. If I were the President, instead of spending twenty billion dollars to go to the moon, I would spend twenty billion dollars and clean up every ghetto in the United States.

You say you are free intellectually. Two plus two is four; it is never five. We are free within certain limitations. I have freedom, but I do not have freedom to hit you in the nose. Freedom has responsibilities, and with freedom comes certain responsibilities and rules and regulations.

Einstein once said, "I feel like a man chained. I get a glimpse of reality and then it flees. If only I could be free from the shackles of my intellectual smallness, then I could understand the universe in which I live."

Some people want moral freedom. We have a period today when we have free love in sex expressions. And we think we are free. But the paradox is, the more free love we have and the more sex expression we have, the more frustrated we become. It is making us miserable. With all of our freedoms, we are beginning to find out that something is missing. We do not have real freedom because these so-called freedoms bring new kinds of bondage, new kinds of tyranny that grip us and may ultimately destroy us.

Men are seeking today for social freedom, freedom from ignorance, freedom from want, freedom from fear; and then they are ignorantly seeking religious freedom. We are hearing many voices in America today that say that religious freedom means that we are free from God. We have a small but aggressive group of people in America today that wants to throw God and the Bible out of the schools. I tell you that our forefathers never meant that we were to have freedom from God. They meant us to have freedom from religious tyranny but not freedom from God.

In America we have four religious faiths. We have Protestantism, Catholicism, Judaism, and now a fourth—secularism. We now call ourselves the pluralistic culture. Secularism is the fastest growing religion in America. It is both a faith and a religion. Even though it claims it wants to throw off the shackles of religion, it in itself has become a religion; and many people are more fanatical and dogmatic in their secular faith than religious leaders have ever been.

This is the cry of everyone today—freedom! I heard the other day about some "free thinkers" who threw a man out of their society because he persisted in faith in God. What freedom this was! Jesus Christ said, "Ye shall know the truth, and the truth shall make you free." And all men are seeking the truth today. Scientists are seeking truth about the physical universe, philosophers are seeking to explain the reason why we are here and the meaning of life. Psychologists are looking for truth about the mind, its action and reaction. And yet we never seem able to come to the truth. That is why Buddha, the great religious leader of the East, said at the end of his life, "I am still searching for truth."

Here is man, for thousands of years searching, studying, wanting to know truth, and he does not seem any closer to ultimate truth today than he was hundreds of thousands of years ago. We have not made much progress in our philosophy from the days of Aristotle, and Plato, and Socrates. Buddha said, "I am still searching for truth." And the average philosopher would say the same thing today. In fact, John Paul Sartre, the great French Existentialist, has said, "It is hopeless. We cannot find ultimate truth. It eludes us." It was Jesus Christ who said, "Ye shall know the truth, and the truth shall make you free." Paul wrote of such ones, "Ever learning, but never able to come to a knowledge of the truth."

Where do you find the truth? If you knew it, it would free you, it would change your world, it would change your home, it would change your community, it would change your life. But what is the truth? This is the question Pilate asked. He asked Christ, "What is truth?" Then Jesus Christ said something very astounding and amazing that shook the people of his day from one end to the other, and shakes me every time I think about it, and should shake you. Jesus Christ made the astounding statement, "I am the truth." Think of it a moment—one man daring to stand before his contemporaries and say, "I am the embodiment of all truth. I am the truth. I am ultimate truth. I am the truth that the philosopher is searching for. I am the ultimate truth back of the physical universe. I am the truth back of what the psychologists are searching for in the understanding of the mind. I am truth." Now Jesus Christ was either a deliberate deceiver who knew he was not the truth, or he was a maniac that should have been in a mental institution, or he is truth. Which is it? Do you think he was a liar? Do you think he was crazy? Or do you think he is the truth? He said, "I and the

Father are one. No man cometh to the Father but by me." He said, "No one will get to heaven except by me."

And that is the decision you have to make. That's the intellectual decision you have to make. That is the decision I had to face as a student when I gave my life to Christ. I had to decide who he was. I finally realized I could not decide intellectually alone. I had to take the ultimate step by faith. When I finally decided that I would accept Christ by faith as ultimate truth, everything else in life fell into place. My intellectual questions were satisfied. A deep need in my soul was satisfied. I found the peace, the security, the relaxation and joy in this faith that I had never known before. It has lasted and has grown and intensified through the years. Now I have the answers to the great questions which the philosophers are asking, not because I am more clever than they are, but because I have accepted by faith that Jesus Christ is the answer to the jigsaw puzzle of the mystery of man. He had the answers; and Christ told the truth. He told the truth about sin, the moral disease that grips the hearts of people. He said, "For from within, out of the heart of men, proceed evil thoughts, adulteries, fornications, murders, thefts, covetousness, wickedness, deceit, blasphemy, pride, foolishness. All these evil things come from within, and defile the man." In other words, Jesus said, "It is not the social problems that are your real problems. It is not a lack of education, not a lack of civilization. The real problem is inside of man." He said that more than nineteen hundred years ago, and if that were not the problem, man himself would have solved his dilemma by now.

I have read some of the articles that were written at the turn of the century. They said that the nineteen hundreds—"the Christian Century"—was going to bring in the millennium. There would be no more wars. Many articles were written exclaiming that mankind had progressed beyond war! Now we have had two devastating wars and we stand on the brink of a third one with terrifying weapons that could destroy civilization. You would think that man would solve these problems and get better, but instead he seems to be getting worse. Did you know that murder in Los Angeles County, for example, increased in the first six months of 1963 by sixty per cent over 1962? Rape, immorality, wickedness, sadism are increasing. But Christ said, "It comes from within." He said, "Inside of us is a disease, and it pours forth like a sewer in pride, hate, jealousy, lying, lust, greed." He said that everyone of us is affected. We were born with a tendency, with the ability to sin. When we reach the age of moral accountability, we all deliberately sin just like Adam did. We have broken the moral law. We are sinners by birth and by personal choice.

Yes, we are free. Everyone of us is free. We are free moral agents. You have a will of your own, but we all deliberately choose to break the laws of God and everyone of us is guilty. Each one of us has a beast inside of us that is ready to jump at any moment. We are sinners. Christ told the truth about that. He also told the truth about judgment. He warned the people about the wrath of God. The Scripture says, "But I say unto you, That every idle word that men shall speak, they shall give account thereof in the day of judgment." Jesus also said, "The men of Nineveh shall rise in judgment with this generation, and shall condemn it, because they repented at the preaching of Jonah; and, behold, a greater than Jonah is here." Jesus said there will be a time of judgment.

Jesus talked about something else more than all the writers of the Bible put together. Jesus talked about hell. Jesus didn't say there is no hell. Jesus said there is a hell. He said there is a life after death and he gave illustrations and stories about it. He said that after you die you will live in heaven or in hell. Jesus described hell, and he warned us not to go there. He said it would be better if your eyes offend you to pull one out, rather than go through life with two eyes and go to hell. He described hell in most graphic terms—it is separation from God. He said men shall have to give an account before God. He said every word that you speak and every thought that you think from the time you are born will be given an account of at the judgment of God and will be weighed in the balances of God's judgment.

Now, did Jesus lie, did he misrepresent, did he deceive us? Or is there a judgment? I tell you on the authority of the Bible, we are all moving toward judgment, that there is a heaven and a hell. Jesus talked about a future life in which we will be more alive than we are now.

Then Jesus told the truth about repentance. He said, "Except you repent, you shall perish." You will perish if you do not repent. Have you repented? Has there been a moment in your life when you really repented of your sins? Repentance is not just saying, "I am sorry." Repentance is not just saying, "Yes, I have sinned." That's a part of it. But it is turning from your sins, it is giving them up, it is allowing God to come in and disturb and change your life and reconstruct your life. Repentance means a change takes place in your life. You turn from sin to Christ. Your mind is changed. Your heart is changed. Everything about you is changed. That is repentance. Have you repented? You can now.

Notice, you must be willing to repent. You may not know how

to repent. You may not be able to repent, but God helps even in our repentance. He will help you now.

And Jesus told the truth about conversion. He said, "Except ye be converted and become as little children, ye shall not enter into the kingdom of heaven." Now is that true enough? Think of it now —except ye be converted and become as little children ye shall not enter into the kingdom of heaven. Psychiatrists have told me that they are converting people, psychologically speaking. But Jesus talked about something more profound and total. You must turn from your way of living to a new way of living. You must turn from sin as the road that leads to destruction, to the narrow road that leads to eternal life. This is conversion; it is a change, it is a turnaround.

How long does it take to be converted? Well, there may be a long process in which you are concerned about it. You have thought about it, you have had opportunity, you have put it off. But then there must be a moment sometime, somewhere to say "Yes" to Christ, a moment of commitment, whether it is conscious or unconscious. There is a moment—a moment to decide, a moment when you stand at the crossroads. There are two roads before you now, two masters, two destinies. You have to make up your mind. And when you decide to go Christ's way, the narrow way, that is conversion.

Now, it is not necessarily emotional. In fact, there may be no emotion at all. When I came to Christ there was no great emotion. I did not cry. It was just a simple act of my will in which I said, "Yes, Lord Jesus, come in." It was a simple thing, and it is so uncomplicated that many people stumble. I wish I could show you this. It is so simple that a little child can understand it. That is why Jesus said, "You have to come as a little child." Even the intellectual, the professor, must come as a little child and trust in Christ. That is conversion.

Jesus told the truth. Do you believe that? I know you believe that much. But what does the truth do? Ye shall know the truth and what? The truth shall set you free. Oh, if you knew Christ, he would set you free. You may be in a jail, but you are free. You may be living in the Soviet Union, but with Christ in your heart you are free. Free from what? First, you are free from the penalty of sin. The Bible says there is a judgment and there is a hell. There is a hell in this life for the person that disregards moral law and sins against God. There are many of you who do not have peace, joy and happiness in your life. You have no real security. You may have a good job, you have a happy family, but there is something lacking down inside. You are missing something. Give your life to Christ. Let him free you from the power of sin in this life and the presence of sin in the life to come.

You say, "Well, Billy, how can I do it?" By a simple act of your will you can say, "I receive Christ." He will come into your life and do it all for you. That is the beauty of coming to Christ. You do not have to do anything except let him in—that is all. "If thou shalt confess with thy mouth the Lord Jesus and believe in thine heart that God has raised him from the dead, thou shalt be saved." How can you do it? Tell God that you want the freedom from the penalty of sin, the power of sin and, some day, the presence of sin and that you want Christ in your heart. Then publicly make known your decision. Tell it to the whole world. Remember, Jesus Christ hung on the cross for you publicly, and he said, "If you are not willing to confess me before men, I will not confess you before my Father which is in heaven." There is something about an open confession that involves an act of your will. You are saying to God publicly, openly, "I receive Christ as my own." Do so now! Let Christ set you free. Receive him now.

2. H. Leo Eddleman

Getting Down To Business
Mark 8:36

"Let's talk business!" — the really serious kind. Some say, "There's no biz like show biz," but few derive sustenance from such in the hours of crisis, death, and judgment.

A sharp, cutting edge persists in the words, "What does it profit a man, if he shall gain the whole world and lose his own soul?" No preacher can ask himself this question and continue to preach in an indifferent, take-it-or-leave-it attitude. No Sunday School teacher can hold this question in purview and teach on Sundays a half-prepared lesson in a half-hearted manner. No deacon can face this question seriously and without wanting to promote the program of his church. "What does it profit a man if he gain the whole world and lose his own soul?"

>We squander health in search of wealth
>   We scheme and toil and save
>Then squander wealth in search of health
>   And all we get's a grave
>We live and boast of what we own
>   We die and all we get's a stone.

Here we face the issues of Vital Values, Permanent Profits, and Soul-salvation. True ecumenicity requires agreement on basic values.

I. Vital Values

What is really worth-while? What things are worthy of the energy, effort, time, and talent of a man created in the image of God?

A distorted sense of values besets our age. Many things our forefathers sought have been lost sight of. Things they would not set store on are sought as the *summum bonum* of life. The sight of bewildered adults but augments the confusion of young people, who know more than any other generation but do not know what to do with their knowledge, who can travel faster than the youth of any other age but have no idea where they should be going.

It has been rightly said that we live in an age which thinks that being lost in the woods is a new freedom - - -

Which, having made a mess of civilization, petulantly cries, "Why doesn't God do something?"

Which, because it subtracts faith, multiplies fear.

In which men demand education for their children, but decline discipline for themselves.

Which puts the highest premiums on knowledge, but when it gets it, it does not know what to do with it.

Which seems to think it has robbed death of its sting by transforming the cemetery into a "memorial park."

Which boasts of its unbelief, instead of being ashamed.

Which believes religious fakers, and follows religious quacks, but thinks itself too intelligent to accept the Word of God.

Which prepares for everything, even for a "rainy day," but fails to prepare for Judgment Day and eternity.

Now, "What does it profit a man if he shall gain the whole world and lose his own soul?" This question can help us get life back into focus, to regain the true perspective.

A friend shopping in a super-market noticed that the customer just ahead was in an animated argument with the cashier over the price of an article. Claiming that the article was marked only 27¢, she was met with adamant insistence on the part of the cashier that it was 57¢. To settle what could have become a serious quarrel, it was suggested that they go to the section of the store from whence the article was originally selected and see what it was marked. It was soon discovered that some vandal had taken the various markers and mixed them up hopelessly. High price tags were pinned on cheaper products and low ones on the more costly! Hardly any of the commodities were now marked accurately.

Precisely this has happened to the glittering American way of life! Our forefathers hung a high marker over the scriptures — we let our Bibles become dust-covered or permit them to adorn the front room like good-luck pieces in the form of horse shoes over a farm-house door. They prized freedom of worship, daring the stormy Atlantic in sail-boats in order to achieve it—we have reduced it to "freedom from worship." After making due allowance for the excesses of stern Puritanism, we tacitly confess the repudiation of true values when movie houses are filled and sanctuaries empty on Sunday nights. When the lights are off in the church, are they off also in the hearts of the nation's citizens?

In the early months of World War II an afternoon daily reported that one movie star had just had her ankles insured for $15,000 and another her shoulders for $25,000. A column in the paper noted that G. I. Joe, out to risk his life for the spiritual values of democracy, was having his whole life—ankles, shoulders and all—insured by the U. S. Government for only $10,000. A civilization which channels its money thus, reflects a perverted sense of values. Many people are paying big money for cheap articles. Jesus in Mark 8:36 says in effect that one human soul is worth more than all the stock values of Wall Street, than all the gold in Fort Knox.

"For the things which are seen are temporal; but the things which are not seen are eternal. For we know that if our earthly house of this tabernacle were dissolved, we have a building of God, an house not made with hands, eternal in the heavens" (II Cor. 4:18-5:1). "For dust thou art, and unto dust shalt thou return" (Gen. 3:19). The old comparison between the value of a soul and that of a body is still valid even in the age of nuclear energy. The soul will abide forever. The body is a temporary tenement to house the real immortal personality. Yet we spend most of our time and money pampering the body and comparatively little to develop the mind, character, spirit, soul. That is not good business; it is not good religion; it is not the teaching of Jesus.

German scientists once subjected a human body immediately after death to an experiment designed to compute its real value. The body was chemically decomposed so that all the various elements could be separated into vials. When it was completed, there was about enough potash to fertilize a small hill of potatoes once, enough water to moisten it for a few days, enough iron to make a few pins, enough iodine to treat one small bruise; other elements were in comparable quantities. The experiment showed that an average human body could bring on the market just 87½¢. Men pay fabulous sums to coddle, pamper and thrill an 87½¢ body. The obituary of a deceased man sometimes states he was "worth" several millions. He was worth exactly what any of the rest of us are, 87½¢ and no more.

And the value of the soul? Jesus held it along side all the material wealth of the universe and said one soul is worth more than all wealth. What does it profit a man if he gain all the money in the world and lose his own soul? What does it profit a woman if she shall climb to the highest rung on the social ladder and lose her own soul? What does it profit a young man if he gain all the power there is and die a lost soul? What does it profit a young girl if she becomes more pouplar than all others and at last loses her soul? A consideration of Jesus' most penetrating question may bring among Christians a more profound oneness of concern, and not only for unbelievers, but for the nurturing of all who are joined to the body of Christ in his Spirit and teachings.

II. Permanent Profits

This text pulls back the curtain from before the future. It looks at ultimate values. Will the investment in Christian living be justified in coming years? It is at this point that the cause of Christ insists on being heard. When the span of life is over, what investments will still have value, will continue to bring satisfaction?

A good deacon (there is seldom any other kind) once came to me and said, "Preacher, I feel like a failure. I've won only two boys in my class to Christ this year." With arm around him I offered these words of encouragement, "Why, brother, that means you have succeeded! Many men in our city are investing heavily in night club and distillery stock and are temporarily succeeding. But remember, they are succeeding in projects that will ultimately fail completely. As God's kingdom succeeds, their businesses will fail. To some you may seem to have failed, but actually you have had at least a small measure of success in the one eternal, victorious business of the universe — the kingdom of God. Don't forget Woodrow Wilson's words to his friends on his last birthday, 'I had rather fail in a movement that will ultimately succeed, than to succeed in a movement that will ultimately fail.' "

This is God's business text. Some opine that religion is often impractical. But while "good business may not always be good religion, good religion is always good business." This text speaks of "profit," "loss," "gain." It is "strictly business," as though it were saying, "Come now, let's get down to business; be practical, be realistic. What is a man *profited* if he shall *gain* the whole world and *lose* his own soul?"

This question makes theology real and meaningful. Has sin robbed man of his glory? Then he can accept the provision God has made for the salvation of his soul. In his death on Calvary's cross Christ took the punishment for every man's sins. I could not understand how his blood shed 1900 years ago can benefit me. But God said it was so. Others insisted it was so. I tried it and now I believe it is so. Millions confirm the divine-human encounter every decade. Empirical and experiential, salvation by faith in Christ often defies theory. Its doctrinal expression may enrich and strengthen it, but the experience is the essence of reality to the believer.

The fellow eking out a living in Arabia could not understand how a mechanical invention thousands of miles away years ago could give value to a black, foul-smelling liquid gushing out of the midst of his sand dunes. He finally ceased questioning the mystery involved, accepted the proposition of a great American oil firm and proceeded at once to enjoy the benefits of better housing, food, medical facilities and education. The benefits of the oil of God's grace in Christ Jesus are even more accessible to the man who will make a studious, business-like approach to the issues of salvation, life, death, sin, righteousness, heaven, hell. "What is a man profited if he shall gain the whole world and lose his own soul?"

III. Soul-Salvation

An eminent church leader recently said that Christianity ought to change its terminology, that the world could no longer understand it. The man's opinion deserves consideration. But is it not a church's responsibility to familiarize the world with the language of the written record of the Christian revelation?

Good phrases sometimes fall into disrepute. Some words have no good synonyms. God's word for sin is sin, for example. "Salvation of the soul," "forgiveness of sin," "the conviction of the Holy Spirit," "being born again," are old-fashioned terms. Actually they convey values beyond the power of the human mind to compute. Jesus spoke to Peter about being "converted"—a word often loathed by a sophisticated age. Yet to be "converted" to Christ Jesus from a life of sin and unbelief is the most dynamic experience which can come to man. Paul, a violent persecuter, was soundly "converted" (Acts 9:1-6) and became the world's outstanding Christian. He was not simply converted to an institution or church, prating and advertising the fact for the sake of political or social advantage: he was converted to Christ, to a life of obedience to his cross. He became a man of broad sympathies and fine sensibilities toward the entire human family. He was trenchant in speaking his convictions but always ecumenical in outlook and spirit. The false teacher undermining the lordship of Christ incurred his wrath, while the least acts of kindness by faithful men he cherished and commended (II Tim. 1:16; 4:11).

A time comes to every man when he would rather know that

he is a saved soul than to have a million dollars. When the last whistle is blown and the last play is being completed, the assurance that one will be received into the Lord's presence is dearer than all earth's wealth. The very things we have pursued in life but which have come between us and Christ will become loathsome and worthless in the final hour. The besetting sin, the pride of mind that kept faith out, the raucous night spots, the hilarity of lustful living are no staff or stay when crossing the river of death. They are even repulsive as well as worthless in our hours of greatest need.

When American soldiers were being pushed off Bataan in those dreary months of 1942, the command had come to destroy all cash money on the island lest it fall into the hands of the Japanese. As the break-through came, the money — counted into the millions— was ignited. Hundred, thousand, twenty, ten, five-dollar bills were going up in smoke. Millions, but worthless, as Americans prepared to surrender! One soldier pulled out a burning twenty-dollar bill, lighted his pipe with it and tossed it nonchalantly back into the fire. "Well, boys," he said, "I always did want to light my pipe with twenty dollar bills. Now I've done it." Money in the millions, but worthless, the very thing which many strive after even at the cost of character, friends, principle, health, yea, and salvation itself.

How loathsome in the last hour is that object which has robbed a man of eternal life! When a lost man is buried, the agony of loved ones almost defies comfort. Grief-stricken members of a family seek for the least evidence that their dead loved one had in some measure accepted Christ by faith. No more pitiful sights does a pastor ever see than those cases in which the vestiges of hope are scarce. How different when a pure sacrificial servant of Christ passes on.

The writer had the privilege of preaching in the Colaba Baptist Church of Bombay, India, in January, 1941. The English pastor, Rev. Stone, baptized an Indian woman at the close of the service. Afterward I encouraged him, "Congratulations on the baptism of your convert tonight."

"But she is not 'my convert,' " said the pastor modestly.

"Then whose is she?"

"Adoniram Judson's," came the reply.

"But Judson lived over a hundred years ago, more than a thousand miles away from here in the country of Burma," I remonstrated.

"True, but this woman fell into the company of a group of women from that city in Burma in which Judson did his most intense suffering and work last century. You recall how he was imprisoned, physically harmed, placed on a starvation diet, and persecuted almost beyond description. Well, these women are descendents of people who were converted by the incomparable life and outstanding witnessing of Adoniram Judson last century. The woman whom I baptized tonight fell into their company and after a few days she came to me saying, 'These Burmese have convinced me that Christ is Savior. I'm ready to be baptized.' You see — she is Judson's convert."

In this life sometimes, as well as in eternity, the blessings of God upon those who labor in his vineyard are evident. "The best of two worlds" comes to him who is captured by Christ and then pours out his life in attempting to capture others for him.

You do not merely have a soul; you *are* a soul. Whatever the distinction between body, soul, and spirit, the indestructible essence of human personality will continue forever. The two alternatives presented by Christ and the New Testament are eternal salvation or eternal condemnation. Salvation in him can be yours; but it is not a cheap salvation. Your decision is one of faith, one of absolute commitment to him as Lord and Savior. Will you make that commitment? Even now before you put this book down, you could resolve in faith to make the doing of his will your primary business in life from now until you meet him face to face.

3. *Gregory Walcott*

WHO IS A CHRISTIAN
John 3:1-16

Today we live in an age where we go by brands and labels and pedigrees. "Christian" is a label given to some people. I am afraid that the term "Christian" or "Christianity" has been used so loosely that we really do not understand the true significance of what it means to be a Christian. Who is a Christian? If I were to ask you, who is a Rotarian, or a Shriner, or a Mason, or Jaycee, or Kiwanian, you could probably tell me. But can you tell me who a Christian is? If I were to go to the main part of town and ask twelve different people on the street to give me their definition of a Christian, I would probably get twelve different answers.

Some time ago, my wife and I put an ad in our local paper that read, "Room free in exchange for services by Christian lady." My wife and I had in mind getting some sweet, motherly, Baptist lady to come and live with us and help us with our children. You should have seen the conglomeration of women who answered that ad! We asked this question of each one, "Are you a Christian?" One particular lady, sensing my probing, asked me, "What do you say a Christian is?" I answered, "I will tell you, but you tell me first." She shrugged and said, "A Christian is anybody who is not a Jew or an Oriental."

I heard a high school teacher make this remark in a devotional, "We are all Christians if we live in America, because America is a Christian nation." When I was a little boy, I thought it was most unusual to hear someone say that so-and-so was not a Christian, because as a lad I just took it for granted that all people were Christians. This is the most tragic delusion in America today—that many, many people are taking it for granted that they are Christian, and that when they die, they will end up in the "happy hunting ground" or the "sweet by and by."

Now, wait a minute, Gregory. You are trying to make it appear that a Christian is a unique person. Certainly I am, because the Bible says that a Christian is a unique person, an unusual person, a distinctive person, a person who is set apart from the society in which he lives. Some people feel that just to attend church makes them Christians. As Dr. Louis Evans has said, "You can no more become a Christian by merely sitting in church than you can become a chicken by sitting in a chicken house." Christianity is not merely a standard by which to live; it is not some hypothetical interpretation of life; it is not some mystical crutch for the weak to wistfully cling to; it is not some checking off of a daily routine existence; it is not some measuring-up process. Christianity is a life! The Bible tells us that the only way to have this life is in a person—the Lord Jesus Christ. Jesus said that the only way to have this life is to be born again. This is the definition of a Christian, according to God's Word — a person who has been born again, who has had a new birth, a new beginning.

Do I hear someone say, "Preacher, you sound 'way out.' What do you mean when you say I must be born again?" Nicodemus asked Jesus this identical question. He said, "You mean that I, a very old man, a very religious man, before I can go to heaven, must be born from my mother again?" In essence, Jesus told Nicodemus that he was rationalizing, thinking in physical terms; that God's kingdom was a spiritual kingdom, and the only way to have entrance into this kingdom was to be born again, to have a spiritual metamorphosis. Of course, Nicodemus asked the obvious question, "Well, how can this happen?" Jesus reminded Nicodemus of a story with which he was familiar. He said in effect, "Nicodemus, you remember how the Children of Israel while in the wilderness were bitten by those fiery serpents and were dying. God instructed Moses to mold, to build a brazen serpent and to lift it high on a pole. Then, if all those people who had been bitten by the snakes would look at the brazen serpent, they would be healed and would live." In a sense Jesus was saying that we, just like the Children of Israel, have been afflicted with a poison not of the body but of the soul.

Now, what is this poison of the soul that affects man's relationship with God, that hinders him from being God's child? Man is afflicted with a poison that the Bible calls sin. Some men deny this; they do not feel that they have sinned. However, God who knows us better than we know ourselves declares that all have sinned. God sees into the innermost depths of our hearts, our consciences, our minds. God knows every thought which we think. God sees us as we really are, and God says of every man, "You are a sinner." When a man is honest, he says to himself and to God, "I am a sinner." This, then, is the first step toward that born-again nature, to acknowledge that we stand before God sinners and in need of salvation.

The question should arise in every lost man's heart, "How can

I get rid of my sins? How can this poison be removed from my soul?" Here is the good news of the gospel. Just as God provided the brazen serpent for the healing of the snake bites, even so God has made provision for the healing of man's sins. "For God so loved the world, that he gave his only begotten Son, that whosoever believeth in him should not perish, but have everlasting life." God gave his Son to bear our sins. The serpent was lifted up on a pole for the healing of the snake bites. Jesus Christ was lifted up on the cross for the healing of man's sins.

Now, I am sure that some of those Israelite grandmothers just knew that they could heal any kind of snake bites. Why, they had had their mustard plasters, their poultices, their ointments, their herbs. They had good old stand-by family home remedies for snake bite. Yet no matter how many of these they applied, the people still died. It was not until they had laid aside their home remedies and cures and looked to God's provision, which was the uplifted brazen serpent, that the bitten people were healed. Even so, before God can heal us of our sins, we must lay aside all of our own ideas of salvation, our "mercurochromed" righteousness, our "antiseptic" piety, our "church-anity." We must throw out all home remedies of salvation, and look only to Jesus Christ, who is God's remedy, God's gift of salvation. It is not until then that God can cleanse us and save us and give us eternal life. This, then, is the second step toward that new birth experience which Jesus required, that we receive God's remedy, Jesus Christ.

You know, when a baby is born, a miraculous thing happens at the moment of birth. Prior to birth, even though the little heart has been beating, all the other organs have not been functioning, but at the exact moment of birth a phenomenon happens. All the little organs begin functioning in synchronization with each other. Now, the doctor could not do this; even the mother could not do this. It is the mystery of life that takes hold at that vital, strategic moment that causes birth and life, and no one can explain it.

In a great sense this is what happens when a person becomes a born-again Christian. He knows that he stands before his Creator and God as one who is lost. And when he goes to God's provision, Jesus Christ, and acknowledges his sin, confesses his sin, and repents, turns away from his sin, at that vital, strategic moment a miraculous thing happens. The Spirit of God enters the heart of that repentant sinner and a marvelous, wonderful, beautiful, miraculous work begins. He becomes a twice-born, blood-bought child. It is a miracle, and no one can explain it. But praise God, it works, it works!

Now, what comes to a person who receives Christ, who has this new birth experience? He has a new life; he is a new person. The Bible says, "Therefore if any man be in Christ, he is a new creature." He is a new person. He thinks differently. He has a new perspective and a new purpose. He is a person who has been transformed into a new creature with a spiritual nature. A born-again Christian is a person who knows that Jesus Christ is real because he has had a personal encounter with Christ. He can now share life with Jesus Christ.

Now, some of you young people are going to meet the boy or the girl of your dreams. You will come to the marriage altar and will say to him or her, "I take thee to be my lawfully wedded wife or husband. I promise to love thee from this day on, etc." What you are saying in essence is this. "I am not going to date my other old boy friends or girl friends any more. I am going to love you only and always. "You know what happens? If you are the girl, you get a new name. You get the man's name. In a sense this is what happens when you become a Christian. You meet Jesus Christ at the altar of salvation. You say to him, "Jesus, by an act of faith I receive you as my sin bearer and Savior and Lord. I promise to live for you from this moment on." What you are saying to Christ is this. "I am not going to live after that old life, those old sins that I used to live and love. I am going to live just for you. I am going to magnify you in my body and through my life from this moment on." And you know what happens? You get a new name. You get His name. You become a Christian. You deserve to be called a Christian.

Some day Jesus will come again. He will not come back as a Savior. He has already come as a Savior. When Christ comes again, he will come as a judge, to judge the sins of the world. When Christ comes, there will be no altar call, no invitation given. The invitation is given now. The Bible says, "Today is the day of salvation; now is the accepted time." And the greatest question you will ever ask yourself is, "Have I been born again?" To you young people I know that the question, "What college shall I go to?" is very important. The question of "What career shall I go into?" is exceedingly important. The question of "What boy or girl shall I marry?" is extremely important. But the most important question that you will ever ask yourself is, "Have I been born again?" For as we are born again, we become the children of God; we become Christians.

Now, in just a moment we are going to extend an invitation. You have an invitation each Sunday. Now what is the invitation?

What is it for? The invitation is for you to make a decision for Christ. It is given for you to be born again into God's eternal, spiritual kingdom. It is given so that you might make a definite break with sin and self, and make a definite commitment to Christ. The invitation is given for you, so that you might receive eternal life—not from this church, but from Jesus Christ. It is given so that you might go to him by an act of childlike faith, and say, "I receive thee, Jesus, into my heart to be my sin bearer, and my Savior, and my Lord." Jesus said, "I stand at the door and knock. If any man hear my voice and will open the door, I will come in to him." Jesus stands at your heart's door, knocking. Open your heart's door and say, "Jesus, come in. Save me. Give me new life." As you do, he will give you a new life abundant and eternal.

4. Carl E. Bates

Greatness In The Church
Acts 2:37-47

It is often said that a certain church is a great church. I doubt not that across the years this description has been given of this church. I have often wanted to stop and examine the statement, to ask the person who makes it exactly what he means. Because, though there are great churches, as men estimate churches, there are churches which have a standing in the community and favor with all the people which may not be great in God's sight. Generally, when we speak of a great church, we mean that the church has a great set of facilities, or that it has an eloquent preacher, or that it has an exceptional music program, or a finely perfected organizational life. This is often what we mean when we say that a given church is a great church.

I submit to you that a church can be great without having any of these things. I have read to you about such a church of the first century. You will find a description of it recorded in the first chapters of the Book of Acts. It had no building in which to meet. It did not have a trained choir. It did not have a Sunday School or a Training Union. It had no training program and no accredited teachers. There were no finely developed organizations or finely coordinated programs in this church, and yet, by the standard of measurement found in the Word of God, it was a great church. Any church, regardless of the kind of facilities it may have in a city, regardless of a staff of ministers which it may employ, regardless of the kind of organization and program that it may develop, may be a great church if it has the qualities and characteristics which were found in this first church.

I have a deep desire for my church to be a great church. I want it to be written in the record that my church is preeminently great like the church described in the early chapters of the Book of Acts was great. If we are great in that respect, we can be great in every other respect. So, I shall simply direct your attention to some of the qualities of greatness in that first church. There are many qualities which could be considered, but in order to help you remember them, I want to present them under these headings: First, this church was great in its preaching; secondly, it was great in its teaching; and thirdly, it was great in outreaching.

1. It Was Great in Preaching

It has been said about certain churches, "That church will not let a preacher fail." This church, to which I direct your attention this morning, did not let the preacher fail. If a church ever had a problem preacher, this church had one. If you will study the life of the Apostle Peter, he was always, as we say, "shooting off his mouth." I like to characterize him as a man who "ran off before he got hitched up." This is true of many Christians. They are quick to run, but they are slow to pull a part of the load. This is true of some of us preachers. A problem preacher is a burden to the church. I want you to consider that this man was "full of the Holy Spirit of God." The Scripture adds that when he stood up there stood with him a group of divinely called and divinely ordained men. Peter stood up in the midst of the one hundred twenty men and women whose lives had been brought under the control of the living Christ. I care not what you call this Person of the Trinity, the Holy Spirit, the Comforter, or the living Lord; the fact is that he lived within these disciples and they were under his control. Simon Peter stood in the midst of spirit-filled people. My heart aches for the preacher today who has to preach under the burden of impulsiveness and impetuousness and a lack of maturity in his own soul. I can sympathize with that man. My heart aches more deeply for him if his people are not interested in having the control of Christ exercised in their lives. My heart bleeds for him if he finds it necessary time after time to stand in the midst of such people without the God ordained leaders standing with him.

This church was great in its preaching because they had a spirit-filled preacher. But they also had a spirit-filled congregation. They had a united, ordained group of men to stand in the church with the preacher. The events of the day of Pentecost left the people amazed. When the people accused the Christians of being drunk, the Apostle Peter, being filled with the Spirit, proclaimed a message from God. Lifting up his voice, he said, "Ye men of Judea, and all ye that dwell at Jerusalem, be this known unto you, and hearken to my words: For these are not drunken as ye suppose, seeing it is but the third hour of the day. But this is that which was spoken by the prophet Joel; And it shall come to pass in the last days, saith God, I will pour out my Spirit upon all flesh: and your sons and your daughters shall prophesy, and your young men shall see visions, and your old men shall dream dreams:" (Acts 2:14-17). The church in our time has lost its capacity to amaze anybody. Do you amaze anybody? Are you so filled with the Spirit that your actions astonish those about you? These Christians were not drunk with wine; their stimulation came from the Spirit. Peter preached about Jesus whom they had crucified and whom, if they continued in their rebellion against God, they would reject. He closed the sermon by saying to them "that God hath made that same Jesus, whom ye have crucified, both Lord and Christ." (Acts 2:36). The word, Lord, refers to his kingly qualifications. The word, Christ, refers to the priestly, atoning qualifications. You see the results of such preaching. Now when the preacher is filled with the spirit of God, when the church is under the control of the living Christ, when a group of ordained men stand with the preacher, when the congregation supports the message proclaimed, the power of God is upon such preaching and great are the results. For the record says, "Now when they heard this, they were pricked in their heart, and said unto Peter and to the rest of the apostles, Men and brethren, what shall we do?" (Acts 2:37).

I have often had people say to me, as I greet them after a service on Sunday morning, "I cannot understand why people are not being convicted in our church." I can understand why! There is no great conviction because we have not met these New Testament qualifications! When the preacher is filled with the Spirit of God, when the people let Christ, the living Lord, exercise control in their lives, when the ordained body of leaders in the church stand together, when the preacher proclaims the Word of God in the midst of the people, the same thing that happened then will happen again. They were pricked in their hearts and the word "pricked" in the scriptures means "they were laid wide open." Every defense they had raised against this man Jesus was taken down. Under the preaching of the Word of God their guard was knocked down. They were laid wide open. Men and women, listen to me today. We have somehow come to a time when the leaders of our churches, including the preachers, have decided that a program will be projected which is guaranteed to do the work of God, even though this program may have no scriptural qualifications.

We may erect our beautiful buildings, call our brilliant preachers, hear our finely trained choirs, and glory over our perfectly organized groups, but if we miss these qualifications, we have failed and shall fail. This is why there is no conviction under the preaching of God's Word. I ask you today under the probing of God's Spirit to measure our church, your church, my church, by this standard of greatness. When the preaching of God's Word was finished, the hearts of those who believed were open before God. It was a great church in preaching. Is our church great in this respect?

II. It Was Great In Teaching

"And they continued stedfastly in the apostles' doctrine." (Acts 2:42). The word, stedfastly, means that they kept everlastingly at it. They stuck to it! Here is a characteristic of the early church which should characterize the church in our time. They had a "stick-to-it-tive-ness." They stayed by the teaching! You would expect this, because our Lord said to them, "No man, having put his hand to the plough, and looking back, is fit for the kingdom of God." (Luke 9:62). If you are going to put your hand to it, stay with it. If you are going to set yourself to the Kingdom task, stay with it. "Oh," you say, "but you do not know how many trials I have. You do not know how many are against me and how many do not understand. I have reasons for not doing more." Oh, drop your "reasons," take them with you to the place of prayer. Lay them before God and see whether or not God will accept them. If he will, then well and good. If he does not, then away with them! You see, what is actually being said here is that they were broadening the knowledge of Christ, the knowledge of truth. The apostles had been taught of Jesus. Forty days he instructed them in the scriptures. Who is your teacher in the Word of God? The same living Lord who taught them will teach you. When it is said that they continued (they stuck to it) in the apostles' teaching, it means that they wanted to learn more of the eternal truth which the apostles had to share. When the apostles stood up to preach, they spoke because they recognized that the people had so little knowledge of spiritual truth.

This is a great burden on my heart. I would not speak unkindly to the people of God; I would not unduly scold; but today we are ignorant of the things of God. There is a dearth of spiritual knowledge in the church. Not too long ago we ran a survey to try to determine spiritual knowledge of our young people. We asked them questions at the beginning of the series of lessons in the Gospel of John. They are your children and my children, but their answers, assuming that they answered to the best of their ability, will shame every home, every teacher, and the whole church for failure to indoctrinate them in spiritual truths. This is the major reason for our organizational life. Even though we are to have a training school for teachers, I had rather have a teacher skilled in the Word of God who can impart it to others, than to have one with all the diplomas on earth but who cannot teach the Word of God. I want this kind of preacher in my pulpit. I have set myself to do this as long as I am your pastor. If you do not have a taste for the Word of God, I shall pray for God to give you this taste so that you may sit under the preaching of this Book. "They continued stedfastly in the apostles' doctrine." They added to their storehouse of spiritual knowledge. They knew of God's prophecy that one day the earth would be full of the knowledge of God. It will not be so unless you and I are full of it. You and I must share it. Never will it be so if you and I remain as babes in Christ, spiritually immature and spiritually ignorant.

Listen, this was also a problem in the early church. I know this because the writer of the Hebrews says, "For when for the time ye ought to be teachers, ye have need that one teach you again which be the first principles of the oracles of God; and are become such as have need of milk, and not of strong meat." (Hebrews 5:12). Milk is just little, light, airy, perfumed preaching that is so popular in our day. Everyone who uses milk is a baby. He cannot feed himself. He has not learned how to nurture himself in the things of the Spirit. Oh, God, save the little babies in the church. Some have been members for years and years and still cannot go to the Word of God and find the food, the strong meat needed for growth. Therefore, I have set myself to preach this Book, to help you understand the true meaning of this Word. Strong meat belongs to those who are fully mature. The New Testament church was great in teaching. Are we stedfast in the apostles' doctrine?

III. It Was Great In Its Outreaching

The early church was great in its outreach. The Christians were continually "Praising God, and having favour with all the people. And the Lord added to the church daily such as should be saved." (Acts 2:47). Here is one of the first characteristics of a New Testament church. Beginning in its own area it reaches out into the whole world.

Insurance executives and "counselors" know that you will not stay in business six months if you only have returns from old business. If you do not get a certain percentage of new business, you ultimately go out of business. This is the one thing I have been trying to establish in the hearts of the people of our church, the need for us to have an outreach in our city. Only as we have outreach can we add to the church those who should be a part of it. When new people moving into our city may get the impression that our church is not interested in them or does not care about them, we must let the people know of our interest.

Moreover, this first church found favor with all the people. They believed that Jesus lived, that He lived in them, and they lived like Him. Until you and I come to that place, I doubt seriously that we have the right to call ourselves a great church. I want it to be a great church. I want it to be great in preaching. I want it to be great in teaching. I want it to be great in outreaching, and not only in our city but to the uttermost parts of the earth. I want more than anything else for God to reach down and call some of our young people to the mission fields. When parents begin to pray for God to call their children to the mission fields, then will our outreach be intensified. When we are ready to go into the world or into our Jerusalem, our outreach will really begin. As you leave today, go from this place with a prayer in your heart that God will help make our church a great church — great in preaching, great in teaching, great in its outreaching.

Would you let the Spirit of God work within you? Perhaps He would call you to reconsecrate yourself. Perhaps He would lead you into our church to help us reach out? Perhaps He could come into your heart and save you. Come in and help us make our church a truly great church.

5. *H. H. Hobbs*

THE INCAPACITY OF GOD
Matthew 26: 39-42

Is there anything which God cannot do? The popular answer to this question would be in the negative. But is this a true answer? We say that God is omnipotent, meaning that He is all-powerful. But even this truth needs definition. For to be exact we must say that God possesses all power to do any and all things which are *in keeping with His nature and purpose.*

These italicized words qualify the statement considerably. Now let it be remembered that this limitation upon God's power is self-imposed, which means that it is not a defect in God's nature but is an evidence of its perfection. Nevertheless, there are some things which God has determined that even He cannot do.

For instance, He cannot act contrary to His nature and purpose. He cannot violate the moral and spiritual structure of the universe. In short, He cannot deny or contradict Himself. Furthermore, it is impossible for God to be tempted with evil. He cannot lie. Neither can He make wrong to be right. Nor can He make two plus two to equal five. It is morally and spiritually impossible for God to ignore or condone sin, but He must deal with the problem of evil in a manner which is in keeping with His holy and righteous nature, will, and purpose.

It naturally follows, therefore, that God cannot save you from your sin in any manner other than through the atoning work which He has wrought in His Son Jesus Christ. Furthermore, God has ordained that He cannot and will not save you without the consent of your own will. Therefore, it is evident that your redemption involves the interplay of God's will, Christ's will, and your will. Indeed, it is in this light that we may best understand the experience of Jesus in the garden of Gethsemane.

Hear the first prayer which Jesus prayed in Gethsemane. "O my Father, if it be possible, let this cup pass from me: nevertheless not as I will, but as thou wilt." (Matt. 26:39).

This prayer is commonly regarded as reflecting the final temptation of Satan designed to deter Jesus from the cross. But is this actually the case? There is no evidence of the presence of Satan's will in this petition. Rather it involves an interplay between the will of the Father and the will of the Son. Jesus did not say, "Nevertheless not as Satan wills, but as thou wilt." He said, "Nevertheless not as I will, but as thou wilt." Jesus had long since brushed aside Satan's will in favor of God's will. The theme which runs throughout the Gethsemane prayer is that God's will shall be done.

Therefore, we cannot say that this prayer involves a conflict between the wills of Father and Son. Instead, it is the question as to whether or not it is possible that God may will that man may be saved by some method other than by Jesus drinking the "cup." "If it be possible" expresses in the Greek a condition which is determined as fulfilled or as assured to be true. So in effect Jesus prays, "Assuming that it is possible, let this cup pass from me."

Now the question naturally arises as to the meaning of "this cup." It is often assumed that it refers to Jesus' death on the cross. This may be, providing that this death is regarded as more than mere physical dying. Otherwise, we make Jesus to pray a cowardly prayer, and He was no coward. Since that night multiplied thousands of the followers of Jesus have rejoiced to die in His name. Our Lord was no less brave than they were and are. Jesus had known, at least from the beginning of His public ministry, that the cross awaited Him at the end of the way. Six months prior to this time He had begun plainly to tell His disciples that He would die in Jerusalem *and be raised from the dead.* (Matt. 16:21). On His final journey to Jerusalem He had even named the manner of His death as crucifixion (Matt. 20:19), referring shortly thereafter to "the cup that shall drink" (20:22). A little over forty-eight hours before the Gethsemane experience He had named the day of His death (26:2). In the upper room that very night He had sought to prepare the disciples for the awful event (John 14-17). Are we, then, to presume that suddenly He lost His courage and prayed for deliverance from death? Such a presumption is contrary to everything that we know about Jesus.

No, the "cup" was not mere physical death. It was that which His death involved. For Jesus did not die as a criminal who had broken either the laws of God or those of the Romans. Neither did He die as a fanatic to a lost cause. Nor did He die as a martyr to truth. He died as a sacrifice for the sins of the world. He gave His life vicariously as God's substitute for a sinful race. It was from this that Jesus drew back in horror.

Now we make no pretense at understanding this. You may ask, "But did not Jesus understand from the beginning that this was involved in His death?" We can only answer in the affirmative. But here it is. "If it be possible, let this cup pass from me."

However, while we cannot understand this, we can at least try to analyze it.

In Romans 3 Paul makes a very evident declaration. "For all have sinned, and come short of the glory of God" (v. 23). "The glory of God" suggests God's holy and righteous nature. So man's sin had violated the very nature of God. Elsewhere the apostle says that "the wages of sin is death; but the gift of God is eternal life through Jesus Christ our Lord" (Rom. 6:23). The Bible teaches that God created man for the purpose of personal, mutual fellowship. However, sin separated between God and man. Therefore, the fellowship was broken. For this reason man was lost from God. He abode in the state of spiritual death or the separation of his soul from God. Was man to remain in this condition which would mean the defeat of God's purpose? Certainly not! For God had willed in eternity and moved in time to redeem man from his son and make possible his restoration to a state of fellowship with God.

This purpose of God Paul declares in his words "Being justified freely by his grace through the redemption that is in Christ Jesus" (Rom. 3:24). Since man was unable to restore this fellowship by law, God willed to do so "by his grace." Doctor C. E. Autrey reminds us that "grace" means that God has done for man what neither he nor anyone or anything else could do for him. While justification is bestowed "freely" or *free for nothing* on man's part, it was by no means free on God's part. It was provided "through the redemption that is in Christ Jesus."

Redemption implies a *ransom*. So to whom was the ransom paid? Obviously not to Satan, or else Satan would be superior to God. No, God paid the ransom to Himself in that He acted to satisfy the demands of His holy and righteous nature. This He did through Christ "that he might be just, and the justifier of him which believeth in Jesus" (v. 26).

God must act in keeping with His nature and purpose. He is holy, and so could neither ignore nor condone man's sin. He is righteous, and so must be just. And "the wages of sin is death." But God is also love. So He could not leave man hopelessly in His sin. How, then, could God be true to His holy nature? He is righteous, so He condemned sin and the sinner. He is love, so He took man's sin upon Himself and bore its penalty that He might redeem man from sin by satisfying within Himself the demands of His holy, righteous, and loving nature. Thus on the cross He was both "just, and the justifier of him which believeth in Jesus."

So much for the fact. But how did God accomplish this? For our answer we turn to 2 Corinthians 5 where Paul says that God "hath reconciled us to himself through Christ" ("Jesus" not in best manuscripts, v. 18). For "God was in Christ, reconciling the world unto himself, not imputing (putting down to account as a charge) their trespasses unto them . . . For he hath made him (Christ) to be sin for us, who (Christ) knew no sin; that we might be made the righteousness of God in him" (vv. 19, 21). Literally, "the one not knowing sin by experience, on behalf of us sin he made, in order that we might become a righteousness of God in him." He made Him not *sinful* but *sin*. He was made sin that we might be made righteousness. Someone has said that Jesus became all that we are that we might become all that He is. He became all that God hates that we might become all that God loves.

It is against this background that we may understand Jesus' first prayer in Gethsemane. All of the sin in the universe was in the cup which the Father offered to the Son. To drink it meant to become completely identified with it. We may not wonder that His sensitive, sinless self drew back in horror from it. He was not any less God when He did so. Rather it was His perfect Divine-Human nature expressing His revulsion at such a nauseous brew. But notice that He did not refuse to drink it. He simply prayed, "Assuming that it is morally and spiritually possible, let this cup pass from me." Yet in the same breath He prayed. "Nevertheless not as I will, but as thou wilt."

But it was not possible. For even God Himself cannot arbitrarily make wrong to be right. He can do so only as He satisfies the demands of His moral and spiritual nature as holiness, righteousness, truth, and love.

The redemption of man involves not only the will of the Father but also the will of the Son. This is seen in Jesus' second (and third) prayer in Gethsemane. "O my Father, if this cup may not pass away . . . except drink it, thy will be done." (Matt. 26:42).

An examination of this prayer is most revealing. Actually it contains two conditional clauses. The first is "if this cup may not pass away." In the Greek it expresses a condition which is determined as fulfilled or assured as true. It is the same condition as that in verse 39 ("If it be possible") except that it is stated in the negative. Thus Jesus is assured in His spirit that it is not possible that the cup may pass away. The second condition is stated in the words "except I drink it." Here the condition is one which is undetermined, but is likely to be fulfilled. He had not yet drunk the cup but the likelihood is that He will do so. The redemptive will of the Father and Son are one. And since there is no other way of redeeming man, there is every likelihood that the Son will drink the cup. That likelihood became a reality as He said, "Thy will be done."

As the Father did not arbitrarily forgive sin, neither did He arbitrarily send His Son to the cross. The cross was eternally in the center of the will of the Triune God. For forgiveness was in God's heart before sin was in the heart of man.

Revelation 13:8 speaks of "the Lamb slain from the foundation of the world." So redemption or the redemptive will was in the heart of God in eternity even before He had created man. Yet that which was wrought in eternity must be accomplished in history. Hence the incarnation of God in Jesus. This involved the will of the Son as well as that of the Father.

This truth is set forth in Hebrews 10:4-7. The author links eternity with time when he says, "For it is not possible that the blood of bulls and of goats should take away sins. Wherefore when he (Christ) cometh into the world, he saith, Sacrifice and offering thou wouldest (willed) not, but a body hast thou prepared me . . . then said I, Lo, I come (in the volume of the book it is written of me,) to do thy will, O God."

This will Jesus did perfectly throughout His sojourn on earth. In so doing He not only fulfilled God's righteousness but He justified God before man. For He demonstrated in His life that it is possible for one to endure every kind of temptation, yet without sin. Thus He showed that God is just in His righteous demands. So having justified God before men, He now must make possible man's justification before God. Thus He takes the cup of sin to drink it, to become sin, that on the cross God may be in Christ reconciling the world unto Himself.

While we cannot fully fathom His cry of desolation on the cross, we know that in that moment He was forsaken even of God that alone He might tread the winepress of God's wrath against sin. It was for only a moment. But in that moment the infinite God suffered infinitely for the sin of a lost world.

Just before He dismissed His spirit Jesus cried, "It is finished" *(tetelestai)*. This one Greek word had many meanings in everyday life of that period (See my *The Crucial Words from Calvary*, Baker, 1958, Chapter 6). But one is most expressive at this point. A father sent his son on a mission, telling him not to return until he had successfully completed it. When he returned he reported to his father, "It is finished" *(tetelestai)*. The heavenly Father sent His Son on the mission of redemption. He drank the cup. He became sin. And now that the penalty for sin had been paid, He cried, *"tetelestai!"* It is finished! Mission accomplished! Matthew 27:50 says that Jesus "when he had cried . . . with a loud voice, yielded up the ghost." Literally, He "dismissed his spirit." His life was not taken from Him. He laid it down of Himself. And He dismissed His spirit only after he had drunk the last bitter dregs of the cup, because His will and that of the Father were one.

In the beginning we noted that man's redemption involves the interplay of the will of God, the will of Christ, and the will of man. Now we have noted the first two as being expressed in the garden of Gethsemane, but there is no mention of the third. However, it is involved nevertheless. It is the responsibility of each of us to inject his own will into the picture. For while it was impossible for God to redeem man apart from the willing sacrifice of His Son, it is equally true that God has willed that He cannot save you apart from the consent of your will.

God made you a personality not a puppet. As a personality you have the right of choice. You can choose to accept or reject God's redemptive work for your salvation. But you are responsible for the choice that you make. God will not violate your personality by coercing you to receive that which He has done in Christ for the forgiveness of your sins. At the same time He has done all that even God can do to make possible your redemption. The rest is up to you.

It is significant, therefore, that the last invitation given in the Bible is "And whosoever will, let him take the water of life freely" (Rev. 22:17). Literally, "the one willing, let him take water of life freely" or as a gift. It is as though the Holy Spirit is saying, "Come, for all things are now ready. God in Christ has made available your redemption. If you are willing you may receive it as a gift." Moreover, God offers it on no other terms. "Forasmuch as ye know that ye were not redeemed with corruptible things, as silver and gold . . . but with the precious blood of Christ, as of a lamb without blemish and without spot" (1 Peter 1:18-19).

Now what does it mean for you to be willing? It means that you must recognize yourself as a sinner lost from God. You must see the death and resurrection of Jesus as God's provision for your redemption from sin. Thus you must repent of your sin, and turn to God in faith through Jesus Christ for forgiveness and for eternal life.

You would do well prayerfully to read over and over again Isaiah 53. Doctor Franz Delitzsch has called it "the Good Friday of the Old Testament." It is as though the prophet was transported over seven hundred years into the future as he stood at the foot of Jesus' cross. Hear him as he rises from one height to another. "He is despised and rejected of men . . . " When Handel, writing *The Messiah,* came to these words, he is said to have been found with his head upon the table, weeping. "Surely he hath borne our griefs, and carried our sorrows." When Charles Haddon Spurgeon read Isaiah 53:5, he said, "I have lost the power to doubt him when I see those wounds."

Doctor G. Campbell Morgan tells a wondrously heart-moving story. Many years ago he heard an old English preacher read Isaiah 53. He read the entire chapter without comment, except for three words interjected between verses four and five. " . . . we did esteem him stricken, smitten of God and afflicted. 'We were wrong!' He was wounded for our transgressions, he was bruised for our iniquities: the chastisement of our peace was upon him; and with his stripes we are healed."

Yes, we were wrong! The word "for" makes all the difference in the world. "For our transgressions . . . for our iniquities" means that the shame, wounds, crushings, and death were not Jesus' but ours. As you see Jesus hanging on the cross you can say, "Except for the grace of God there hang I."

It is when you see Jesus dying in your place and through Him turn to God in faith for salvation that you are "the one willing." He waits for the submission of your will to His saving will to extend to you His almightiness to save.

Yes, God is omnipotent. But in His perfect omnipotence He has bound Himself by certain incapacities. None is so meaningful and glorious as His incapacity to save you apart from the redemptive work which He wrought in His beloved Son Christ Jesus. Neither does God honor you more than in the fact that He wills that He cannot save you against your own will. But to all who submit to Him He is able, willing and mighty to save to the uttermost—from the uttermost of sin unto the uttermost of salvation as He justifies, sanctifies, and glorifies you unto the praise of His glory.

"For God so loved the world, that he gave his only begotten Son, that whosoever believeth in him should not perish, but have everlasting life" (John 3:16).

6. *V. L. Stanfield*

AN INVITATION ESPECIALLY FOR YOU
Isaiah 55:1-3; Matt. 11:28-30; Rev. 22:17

The invitation has become a distinctive part of the worship service in most Baptist churches. Even though it is rarely listed in the printed order of worship, it is considered to be a normal and essential part of the service.

But not all churches have invitations. In fact, many do not. Moreover, some Baptist churches do not have invitations. Some individuals question the practice of having public invitations. Indeed, some people are sharply critical of this practice. Perhaps it would be good for us to raise the question "Why?" Why do we give invitations?

For one reason this practice follows apostolic method. When the apostles had preached the gospel, they said in essence, "Therefore, repent and believe." Simon Peter urged, "Repent ye, therefore, and be converted that your sins may be blotted out." (Acts 3:19a).

Moreover, the invitation is the natural and normal outcome of a gospel sermon. When the preacher has declared the mighty acts of God, it is natural to ask those listening to believe and to let God work in their hearts.

Certainly the spirit of the invitation is found throughout the Bible. This spirit is typified in Isaiah's invitation, "Ho, everyone that thirsteth, come ye to the waters . . . incline your ear and come unto me: hear and your soul shall live." (Isaiah 55:1, 3). It seems not without reason that the last chapter of the last book of the Bible has an all-inclusive invitation. "The spirit and the bride say, Come. And let him that heareth say, Come. And let him that is athirst come. And whosoever will, let him take the water of life freely." (Rev. 22:17).

Above all, we have the example of Christ. When Jesus was in the midst of his earthly mission, he was constantly inviting men and women and boys and girls to come to him. When the disciples would have forbidden the children, Jesus said, "Allow the little children to come unto me, and forbid them not, for such is the Kingdom of God." (Matt. 19:14). To all who were burdened, to all caught in the bondage of sin, Jesus invited, "Come unto me all ye that labor and are heavy laden and I will give you rest." (Matthew 11:28).

Consequently, we have good reason to give invitations. Without any apology we give invitations. We entreat, invite, exhort, plead and beseech men and women, boys and girls to be reconciled with God.

Because the invitation will be a part of each service of this revival, I want to talk to you about the invitations usually given in a Baptist church.

I. Vocational Christian Service

One invitation is the invitation for young people and others to offer their lives in vocational Christian service. This is an invitation to make some area of Christian service the vocation of life.

Now always this invitation must be between each person and God. The call of God must be heard. But I think we need to be saying to our young people, "God has the first call on your life." There are so many things that can be done today by those who will hear God's call and prepare. It has not been many years ago when there were just a few things you could do. You could be a pastor or a missionary. But today there are literally a thousand different things which can be done in vocational Christian service. Not only may you be a pastor, but you may be an assistant pastor, a minister of music, a minister of education, a secretary, a financial secretary, or a teacher. On the mission field, you may not only be a preacher, but a teacher, a doctor, or a nurse. We are even sending out agricultural missionaries who are teaching people how to get bread from the soil; then, they are offering the people the bread of life. In the chaplaincy, you may not only be an armed service chaplain, but you may be an institutional chaplain, or an industrial chaplain. Then, think of our colleges and boards and institutions. So many, many things may be done by those people who will listen to the call of God.

Perhaps in your church, where there are many wonderful young people, the call of God is being heard. Perhaps God has been asking for the lives of young people. A few years ago I was preaching at a meeting in a little Mississippi town. It was not a large church, but I think I have never seen a more mature church. Certainly I have never met more mature young people. During the days of that meeting, one by one, young people responded until fourteen had volunteered for Christian service. Some surrendered to preach, some for missions, one in music; one boy's father ran the local newspaper and this young man came forward saying, "I want to give my life to be a Christian editor." Perhaps God has been asking for your life.

In the years just past we Southern Baptists have been trying to establish thirty thousand new churches and preaching stations. We need seventy-five thousand. When we have them, there will not be men and women to serve them. When we think of our world, a three billion world that will soon be a five billion world, you realize that we are losing the battle. We need ten thousand missionaries. Many of you should consider the call of God to serve him in some vocation. In a few moments, I am going to invite you to offer your life in Christian service. If God has been calling, answer his call.

II. Rededication of Life

Another invitation often given in a Baptist church is an invitation to rededicate or to reconsecrate one's life. Sometimes this invitation is misunderstood, and sometimes it is even resented. Perhaps it is misunderstood because it means different things to different people. To one person rededication means that this person has fallen into open sin; it is known in the community. But for another person it means that this person has drifted into secret sin, though our sins are never as secret as we think. For another person rededication may mean that God has been pushed into a secondary place, and all of a sudden there is the realization of what has happened. "I am not loyal to my church," or "I have not prayed for weeks." "I have not read my Bible." God has been second. For another person, rededication may mean a new vision of service.

Now I may be wrong, but I believe that the invitation that needs to be most accepted in all churches is the invitation to rededication. If you and I really make Jesus Christ the Lord of our lives, we can win our neighbors. I say that realizing that some people do not feel that rededication is a proper invitation. If you do not think it is, just walk through the pages of the Bible, and see how some of God's greatest saints had to rededicate their lives. What about David? David was a man after God's own heart, but he was a man. One day he looked over on the adjoining roof top, and there was a lovely woman, and he desired her. This desire became lust, and lust, adultery, and adultery, murder. But he knew God, and there was a fire of torment within him. Relief came only when he turned to God and confessed his sin. What about Simon Peter? Simon Peter was big and burly and boisterous. Simon had declared, "Lord, others may deny you, but you can count on me." Then came the day when Jesus was seized, and those about said to Simon, "You are one of them." And Simon Peter denied his Lord! You remember that resurrection scene when Jesus asked Simon three times, "Simon, do you love me?" Simon Peter answered, "Lord, you know all things, and you know that I love you." Simon Peter had to rededicate his life. I expect if many of us would look closely within our hearts and would put aside all shame and hypocrisy, there would be the need of drawing closer to our Lord.

A few years ago I conducted a meeting near Oxford, North Carolina. Many people were making decisions. One day the pastor said, "I want to go talk with two young ladies. They are Baptists and should be in our church." We went to visit them and they said, "Yes, we have been to the meetings; we have seen others make decisions, and we plan to bring our letters." But one girl, a high school girl, said, "Pastor, when I come to bring my letter, I want to make a new start."

Now, you can give God too little of your life. But there is not a man or woman or young person here tonight who can give God too much. In a few moments I am going to ask you to consider rededicating your life to the Lord.

III. Transfer of Membership

Another invitation often given in the Baptist church is the invitation to transfer membership, to become an active part of a local church. As far as I know, this may be done in one of three ways—by statement, or by baptism, or by letter.

Now, this is what is meant by statement. A person belonged to a Baptist church. Faith in Christ had been confessed; the confession was followed by baptism. But the membership has been lost. Perhaps records have been destroyed, or the person went to another denomination, or perhaps church discipline was exercised. In our denomination hundreds of people come back home by statement, a statement of their faith and of their baptism. It may be that some of you need to come back and go to work in this church.

Then there are Christian people who come into a Baptist church by baptism. They belong to other groups, but they decide that they should worship and serve in a Baptist church. Generally this happens when there is a strong desire that a family be together in a church. If I had my way, every family would be together in a church. People who talk together about our love, our home, our house, our car, our boy, our girl, should also talk about our church. Several years ago I was supplying in a church in Knoxville, Tennessee. I met a family there; the lady was a loyal, active member of the church; the daughter was a fine young person in the church; the father was a nominal member of another church; the son was a Junior boy who had not yet received Christ. One night this man came forward and said, "Preacher, I want to rededicate my life and I want to join this church." When the boy saw his father respond, he came forward also trusting in Christ. I had the joy of baptizing both of them. Later, I was waiting for a plane in Nashville, Tennessee, and I "bumped" into this man. As we "chatted," I asked, "How are things going now?" He answered, "You know, since we have started going to church together, everything has been better. We have been much happier." Perhaps some of you should be with your family in this church.

Of course, the main invitation for membership is the invitation to transfer one's letter. You belong to a Baptist church, and you simply ask that your letter be transferred. Now, I hope you carry the news out with you. We Southern Baptists brag about more than ten million members. Ten million! But of the ten million more than three million are non-resident. Three million! Every year in this country now twenty percent of the population moves. That means that nearly forty million people move each year. This will cost the Lord millions of dollars and millions of years of service. Because some people will wait three months to transfer church membership, some three years, some ten years, and some never will. After all, a letter is just a scrap of paper! It is a symbol of a spiritual reality. Every Christian should be a vital member of some local church. Now, some of you should be a part of this church. I am going to invite you; indeed, I want to urge and insist that you will become a part of this church.

IV. Receive Christ as Savior and Lord

The primary invitation given in a Baptist church is the invitation to receive Christ as Savior and Lord. When we offer this invitation, we stand in Christ's stead and speak for him. For he said, "The Son of Man has come to seek and to save that which was lost." (Luke 19:10, NASB). "I am come that they might have life, and that they might have it more abundantly." (John 10:10, NASB). So when we ask you to put your faith in Christ and to receive the gift of salvation, we are ambassadors, entreating you in Christ's stead.

Christ can make you happy. Christ can supply what you lack. Christ alone can save you. To wait is to miss only what Christ can give. I have never known anybody who received Christ who was not glad he did. Moreover, I have never known anyone who postponed turning to Christ who, when he received him, did not wish he had done so before.

I once assisted a pastor in a revival who had a rather unusual plan. He planned to baptize each night before the service. He had candidates awaiting baptism; there were many prospects; so in faith he announced baptismal services for each night. (And God added to the church every day.) On the first Sunday morning of that revival a man sixty-five years old confessed his faith in Christ. That night he was baptized. This meant that for the remainder of the revival the man was a Christian and a member of the church. When the revival ended, he was really happy, but in the happiness there was a note of regret. For he exclaimed, "This has been a wonderful week. But I could have been a member of this church twenty-five years ago. Why did I wait?"

Christ has come to save. He will do it the moment you trust him. I want to invite you to open your heart and to receive Christ.

Which invitation do you need to accept? Surely one is especially for you! Has God been calling for your life? Offer it in his service. Do you need to rededicate your life? Surrender yourself completely to Christ. Should your membership be in this church? You need a church home! Why waste even a week of Christian service? Come now! Are you lost in sin? Are you away from God? Trust Jesus Christ as your Savior. Come right now. Say, "Lord, I believe you. I trust you." I invite you to come, the pastor invites you to come, this church is eager for you to come. The Lord loves you and wants you to be a part of his church. He invites you to come.

Come for all things are now ready. Come as we sing.